Lighthouses of Scotland
by Harold Stiver

Copyright Statement

**Lighthouses of Scotland
A Guide for Photographers and Explorers**

Published by Harold Stiver
Copyright 2024 Harold Stiver

License Notes
All rights reserved. No part of this book may be reproduced in any form or by any electronic or mechanical means including information storage and retrieval systems without permission in writing from the author, except by the reviewer who may quote brief passages
Version 1.0
ISBN#978-1-927835-48-7

Index

A Short History of Lighthouses — 8
The Stevensons: Family of Lighthouse Builders — 10

Aberdeen
Girdle Ness (Girdleness) Lighthouse — 14
Aberdeenshire
Buchan Ness Lighthouse — 15
New Kinnaird Head Lighthouse — 16
Kinnaird Head Lighthouse — 16
Rattray Head lighthouse — 17
Todhead Lighthouse — 18
Angus
Bell Rock Lighthouse — 19
Scurdie Ness Lighthouse — 20
Argyll and Bute
Rubha nan Gall Lighthouse — 21
Toward Point Lighthouse — 22
Carraig Fhada Lighthouse — 23
Davaar Lighthouse — 24
Dubh Artach Lighthouse — 25
Lismore Lighthouse — 26
Loch Indaal Lighthouse — 27
McArthur's Head Lighthouse — 28
Mull of Kintyre Lighthouse — 29
Rinns of Islay Lighthouse — 30
Sanda Island Lighthouse — 31
Scarinish Lighthouse — 32
Skerryvore Lighthouse — 33
Argyll and Bute, Killarow and Kilmeny
Ruvaal Lighthouse — 34
Dumfries and Galloway
Mull of Galloway Lighthouse — 35
Corsewall Lighthouse — 36
Crammag Head Lighthouse — 37
Killantringan Lighthouse — 38
Little Ross lighthouse — 39
Southerness Lighthouse — 40
East Lothian
Barns Ness Lighthouse — 41
Bass Rock Lighthouse — 42
Fidra Lighthouse — 43

Fife
Elie Ness Lighthouse — 44
Old Isle of May Lighthouse — 45
Oxcars Lighthouse — 46
Fife Ness Lighthouse — 47
Inchkeith Lighthouse — 48
Isle of May Lighthouse — 49
Isle of May Low Light — 50

Highland
Corran Point Lighthouse — 51
Dunnet Head Lighthouse — 52
Stroma Lighthouse — 53
Tarbat Ness Lighthouse — 54
Vaternish Lighthouse — 55
Ardnamurchan Lighthouse — 56
Cape Wrath Lighthouse — 57
Cromarty Lighthouse — 58
Duncansby Head Lighthouse — 59
Hyskeir Lighthouse — 60
Neist Point Lighthouse — 61
Noss Head Lighthouse — 62
Ornsay Lighthouse — 63
Point of Sleat Lighthouse — 64
Rona Lighthouse — 65
Rua Reidh Lighthouse — 66
Stoer Head Lighthouse — 67
Strathy Point Lighthouse — 68

Highland and Fortrose
Chanonry Lighthouse — 69

Inverclyde
Cloch Lighthouse — 70

Moray, Lossiemouth and Branderburgh
Covesea Skerries Lighthouse — 71

North Ayrshire
Little Cumbrae Old Lighthouse — 72
Cumbrae Lighthouse — 73
Little Cumbrae New Lighthouse — 74
Holy Isle Inner Lighthouse — 75
Holy Isle Outer Lighthouse — 76
Pladda Lighthouse — 77

Orkney Lighthouses
Hoy Sound High Light — 78
Hoy Sound Low Light — 79

North Ronaldsay Lighthouse	80
Dennis Head Old Beacon	81
Start Point Lighthouse	82
Auskerry Lighthouse Brough	83
of Birsay Lighthouse Cantick	84
Head Lighthouse Copinsay	85
Lighthouse	86
Hoxa Head Lighthouse	87
Lother Rock Light	88
Noup Head Lighthouse	89
Pentland Skerries High Light	90
Sule Skerry Lighthouse	91
Tor Ness Lighthouse	92
Outer Hebrides	
Flannan Isles Lighthouse	93
North Rona Lighthouse	94
Tiumpan Head Lighthouse	95
Barra Head Lighthouse	96
Butt of Lewis Lighthouse	97
Eilean Glas Lighthouse	98
Old Monach Lighthouse	99
New Monach Light	99
Ushenish Lighthouse	100
Weavers Point Lighthouse	101
Scottish Borders	
St. Abbs Lighthouse	102
Shetland Lighthouses	
Firths Voe Lighthouse	103
Bressay Lighthouse`	104
Esha Ness Lighthouse	105
Fair Isle North Lighthouse	106
Fair Isle South Lighthouse	107
Foula Lighthouse	108
Muckle Flugga Lighthouse	109
Bound Skerry Lighthouse	110
Fethaland Lighthouse	111
Sumburgh Head Lighthouse	112
South Ayrshire	
Ailsa Craig Lighthouse Lady	113
Isle Lighthouse **South**	114
Ayrshire, Kirkoswald	
Turnberry Lighthouse	115
Thurso	
Holborn Head Lighthouse	116

Tours
Aberdeenshire Tour	117
Dumfries and Galloway Tour	118
East Coast Tour	119
Isle of May Tour	120
North Coast Tour	121
Southwest Coast Tour	122
Glossary	123
Photo Credits	127
Other Books by the Author	128
Index	129

Short History of Lighthouses

There is some evidence of a lighthouse from the 5th century B.C. of Themistocles of Athens constructing a stone column with a fire on top. This was at the harbour of Piraeus, associated with Athens.

However one of most famous and spectacular early structures was the Lighthouse of Alexandria, or the Pharos of Alexandria. It was one of the Seven Wonders of the Ancient World.

The lighthouse was built in the Third Century B.C. in Alexandria, Egypt by Ptolemy II. It stood on the island of Pharos in the harbour of Alexandria and was said to be 110 metres (350 feet) high.

The lighthouse was built in three stages, a large square at the bottom, an octagonal layer in the middle, and a cylindrical tower at the top.

The structure lasted until a series of earthquakes damaged it, with the 1303 Crete earthquake resulting in its destruction.

The Tower of Hercules, in northwest Spain, is modelled after the Pharos Lighthouse.

The first and oldest lighthouse in Scotland is the Beacon which opened in 1636 and survives to this day. It is also known as the Isle of May Light.

It is situated at the highest point of the Isle of May and consists of three floors with the keepers living on the middle floor and a coal basket on top to warn passing ships. The cost of the coal was charged to to the ship owners.

The Stevensons: Family of Lighthouse Builders

Thomas Smith (1753-1815) was the first engineer at what is now the Northern Lighthouse Board. Robert Stevenson served as an assistant to Smith and, at age 19, was entrusted with building Little Cumbrae Island Lighthouse. When James Smith retired, Robert assumed his position as Chief Engineer. Robert Stevenson, his descendants and his father-in-law James Smith, designed most of the Scottish lighthouses for over 150 years. They were involved with the building of 97 lighthouses between 1799 and 1938. The famous writer Robert Louis Stevenson was Robert Stevenson's grandson.

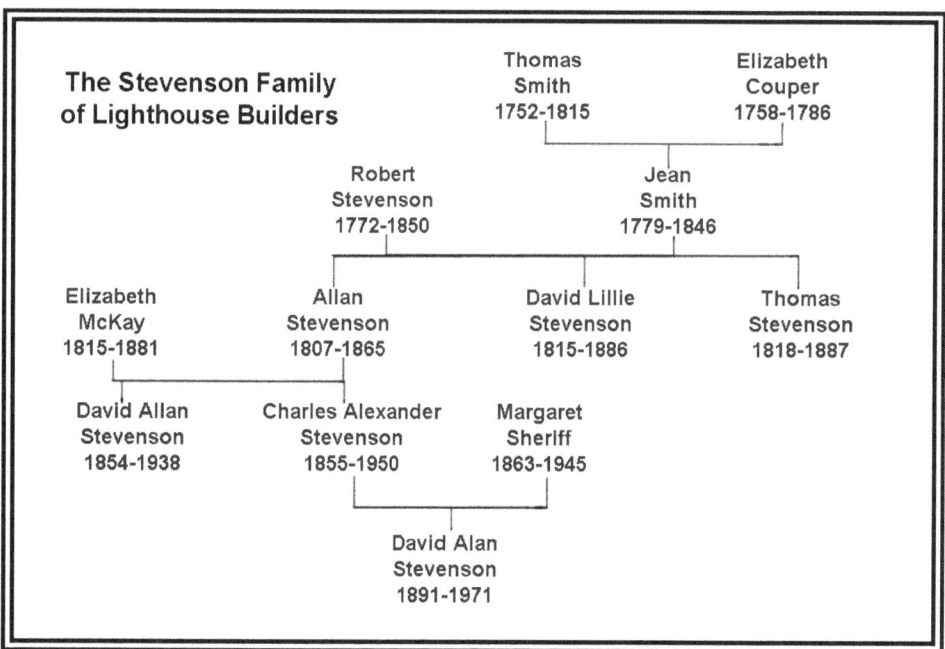

Thomas Smith (1752-1818) was the first Chief Engineer for what would become the Northern Lighthouse Board. He married his third wife Jean Stevenson in 1792. She was Robert Stevenson's widowed mother. Robert became Smith's assistant and later his partner.

Lighthouses engineered by Thomas Smith

Cloch Point*	1797
Eilean Glas	1789
Inchkeith*	1804
Kinnaird Head	1787
Little Cumbrae	1793
Mull of Kintyre	1788
North Ronaldsay	1789
Pentland Skerries*	1794
Pladda	1790
Portpatrick	1790
Start Point*	1806

* with his son-in-law Robert Stevenson

Robert Stevenson (1772-1850) After becoming Thomas Smith's assistant, he was given the responsibility of building Little Cumbrae Lighthouse at age 19. He married Jean Smith, James Smith daughter by his first wife and Robert's stepsister. Among their children where Alan, David Lillie and Thomas who all became engineers of the Board.

Lighthouses engineered by Robert Stevenson

Barra Head	1833	Bell Rock	1811
Buchan Ness	1827	Calf of Man	1818
Cape Wrath	1828	Cloch Point*	1797
Corsewall	1817	Douglas Head	1832
Dunnet Head	1831	Isle of May	1816
Girdle Ness	1833	Mull of Galloway	1830
Lismore	1833	Pentland Skerries*	1794
Point of Ayre	1818	Rinns of Islay	1825
Southerness	1812	Start Point*	1806
Sumburgh Head	1821	Tarbat Ness	1830
Toward Point	1812		

* assisting Thomas Smith

Alan Stevenson (1807-1865) When Alan's father, Robert Stevenson, retired, Alan was appointed as his successor. He was actively involved in designing new lighting apparatus and saw his work used in future lighthouse sites as the standard.

Lighthouses engineered by Alan Stevenson

Ardnamurchan	1849	Arnish Point	1853
Cairn Point	1847	Chanonry Point	1846
Covesea Skerries	1846	Cromerty Point	1846
Hestan Island	1850	Hoy Sound High	1851
Hoy Sound Low	1851	Isle of May	1843
Lismore*	1833	Little Ross	1843
Noss Head	1849	Sanda Island	1850
Skerryvore	1844		

* with his father Robert Stevenson

David Lillie Stevenson (1815 - 1886) When his brother Alan retired as Chief Engineer, David succeeded to the post. He designed thirty lighthouses including some of the most difficult to build.

Lighthouses engineered by David Lillie Stevenson

Auskerry*	1866	Bound Skerry	1854
Bressay*	1858	Butt of Lewis*	1862
Cantick Head*	1858	Chicken Rock*	1875
Corran Point*	1860	Davaar Island	1854
Douglas Head*	1832	Dubh Artach*	1872
Fladda*	1860	Holborn Head*	1862
Holy Island* (inner)	1877	Inchcolm	1858
Kyleakin*	1857	Langness*	1880
Loch Indaal*	1869	McArthur's Head*	1861
Monach Isles*	1864	Muckle Flugga	1854
Ornsay*	1857	Rubha nan Gall*	1857
Ruvaal*	1859	Scurdie Ness*	1870
Skervuile*	1865	South Rona Island*	1857
St Abb's Head*	1862	Stoer Head*	1870
Turnberry*	1873	Ushenish*	1857

* with his brother Thomas

Thomas Stevenson (1818 - 1887) was the brother of Alan and David Lillie Stevenson. He became a partner with them in 1946. He designed over 30 lighthouses in Scotland as well as working on formulations of the action of sea waves on structures.

Lighthouses engineered by Thomas Stevenson

Aisla Craig**	1886	Auskerry*	1866
Bressay*	1858	Butt of Lewis*	1862
Cantick Head*	1858	Chicken Rock*	1875
Corran Point*	1860	Davaar Island*	1854
Dubh Artach*	1872	Douglas Head*	1832
Fidra**	1885	Fladda*	1860
Holborn Head*	1862	Holy Island* (inner)	1877
Inchcolm	1858	Kyleakin*	1857
Langness*	1880	Loch Indaal*	1869
McArthur's Head*	1861	Monach Isles*	1864
Muckle Flugga*	1854	Ornsay*	1857
Bound Skerry*	1854	Oxcars**	1886
Rubha nan Gall*	1857	Ruvaal*	1859
Scurdie Ness*	1870	Skervuile*	1865
South Rona Island*	1857	St Abb's Head*	1862
Stoer Head*	1870	Turnberry*	1873
Ushenish*	1857		

* with his brother David Lillie Stevenson   ** with his cousin David Alan Stevenson

David Alan Stevenson (1854 - 1938) was Senior Engineer of the Northern Lighthouse Board from 1885-1938. Between 1885 and 1886 he built three lighthouses with his uncle Thomas, and then a further twenty-three with his brother Charles.

Lighthouses engineered by David Alan Stevenson

Ailsa Craig**	1886	Barns Ness	1901
Bass Rock	1903	Clyth Ness	1916
Copinsay	1915	Duncansby Head	1924
Esha Ness*	1929	Elie Ness	1916
Fair Isle North*	1892	Fair Isle South*	1892
Firths Voe*	1909	Fidra**	1885
Flannan Isle	1899	Helliar Holm	1893
Hoxa Head	1901	Holy Island* (outer)	1905
Hyskeir*	1904	Killantringan	1900
Maugold Head*	1914	Neist Point	1909
Noup Head*	1898	Oxcars**	1886
Rattray Head	1895	Rubha Reidh	1912
Stroma*	1896	Sule Skerry*	1895
Tiumpan Head*	1900	Tod Head	1897
Tor Ness*	1937		

* with his brother Charles Stevenson   ** with his uncle Thomas Stevenson

Charles Alexander Stevenson (1855 - 1950) was born on 23 December 1855 as 7th child of David Lillie Stevenson and his wife, Elizabeth Mackay. He joined the family business in 1875. As well as building lighthouses. he improved foghorns and worked with optics.

Lighthouses engineered by Charles Alexander Stevenson

Barns Ness*	1901	Bass Rock*	1903
Clyth Ness*	1916	Copinsay*	1915
Duncansby Head*	1924	Esha Ness*	1929
Fair Isle North*	1892	Fair Isle South*	1892
Firths Voe*	1909	Flannan Isle*	1899
Helliar Holm*	1893	Holy Island* (outer)	1905
Hyskeir*	1904	Killanringan*	1900
Maugold Head*	1914	Neist Point*	1909
Noup Head*	1898	Rattray Head*	1895
Rubha Reidh*	1895	Stroma*	1896
Sule Skerry*	1895	Tiumpan Head*	1900
Tod Head*	1897	Tor Ness*	1937

* with his brother David Alan

David Alan Stevenson 2 (1891 - 1971) was the 1st child of Charles Alexander Stevenson and his wife, Jessie McClellan and the fourth generation of the Stevenson family involved in the lighthouse business. Although he did not design lighthouses, he was engaged in maintenance procedures as well as the modernization of equipment.

Girdle Ness (Girdleness) Lighthouse, Aberdeen

Girdle Ness Lighthouse is found on the Girdle Ness Peninsula just south of the entrance to Aberdeen harbour. It was built by James Gibb under the supervision of engineer Robert Stevenson and opened in 1833. Requests for this light had begun in 1813 when the Whaler Oscar was wrecked with only two of the forty four crew surviving. The tower originally supported two lights, one at the top and one part way down. The lower light was discontinued in 1890.

Description: White tower

Location: Aberdeen

Directions: In Aberdeen, head SW on Victoria Rd for 0.8 mi and continue onto St Fitticks Rd for 0.3 mi. Turn left onto Greyhope Rd and in 0.7 mi make a sharp left onto Girdleness Lighthouse Cottage and the lighthouse

Coordinates: 57°08'20.0"N 2°02'55.0"W

Opened: 1833

Automated: 1991

Deactivated: Active

Height: 37 meters, 121 feet

Focal Height: 58 meters, 190 feet

Signal: 2 white flashes every 20 seconds

Foghorn signal: Deactivated in 1987

Visitor Access: Grounds open, tower closed

Buchan Ness Lighthouse, Aberdeenshire

From the Boddam area, trading and whaling vessels sailed and many had met disaster in stormy weather. Calls were made for a lighthouse to the Northern Lighthouse Board and the Buchan Ness Lighthouse opened in 1827. The red band was added in 1897 to aid mariners in identifying their location. The site became private in 2006 and there is rental accommodation for the dwellings available. The light is still active.

Description: White round tower

Location: Boddan

Directions: In the town of Boddam, head southeast on Bridge St from Rocksley Drive and the lighthouse is 800 feet

Coordinates: 57°28'13.0"N 1°46'28.0"W

Opened: 1824

Automated: 1988

Deactivated: Active

Height: 36 meters, 118 feet

Focal Height: 40 meters, 138 feet

Signal: White flash every 5 seconds

Foghorn signal: Deactivated in 2000

Visitor Access: Rental accommodation is available

Kinnaird Head Lighthouse (Old and New), Aberdeenshire

The old and new Kinnaird Head Lighthouses are now part of the Museum Of Scottish Lighthouses exhibit. The original lighthouse was built in 1787 by Thomas Smith, making it the oldest surviving Scottish lighthouse. Smith was the father-in-law of Robert Stevenson, and therefore related to the famous family of lighthouse designers and builders. The new lighthouse opened in 1991 and is still active.

Old

Description: White tower

Location: Fraserburgh

New

Description: White tower

Location: Fraserburgh

Directions: In Fraserburgh, head northeast on Barrasgate Rd from A98 for 0.2 mi and continue straight onto Castle Terrace to find the lights

Coordinates: 57°41'53.0"N 2°00'15.0"W

Opened: 1787

Automated: 1990s

Deactivated: 1991

Height: 11 meters, 36 feet

Focal Height: 15 meters, 60 feet

Signal: Inactive

Foghorn signal: Discontinued 1987

Coordinates: 57°41'51.0"N 2°00'14.0"W

Opened: 1991

Automated: 1991

Deactivated: Active

Height: 10 meters, 33 feet

Focal Height: 25 meters, 82 feet

Signal: White flash every 5 seconds

Foghorn signal: N/A

Visitor Access: Both lights are part of Museum Of Scottish Lighthouses, admission

Rattray Head Lighthouse, Aberdeenshire

The quick red fox jumped over the lazy brown dog. The quick red fox jumped over the lazy brown dog. The quick red fox jumped over the lazy brown dog. The quick red fox jumped over the lazy brown dog. The quick red fox jumped over the lazy brown dog. The quick red fox jumped over the lazy brown dog. The quick red fox jumped over the lazy brown dog. The quick red fox jumped over the lazy brown dog. The quick red fox jumped over the lazy brown dog. The quick red fox jumped over the lazy brown dog. The quick red fox jumped over the lazy brown dog. The quick red fox jumped over the lazy brown dog. The quick red fox jumped over the lazy brown dog. The quick red fox jumped over the lazy brown dog. The quick red fox jumped over the lazy brown dog.

Description: White tower with granite base

Location: Rattray Head

Directions: Take an unnamed road east from Peterhead for 1.0 miles and park at the end. Walk a short distance to the coast where you have a view of the lighthouse.

Coordinates: 57°36'36.0"N 1°48'59.0"W

Opened: 1895

Automated: 1982

Deactivated: Active

Height: 34 meters, 112 feet

Focal Height: 28 meters, 92 feet

Signal: 3 white flashes every 30 seconds

Foghorn signal: 2 blasts every 45 seconds

Visitor Access: Closed, the onshore keeper's dwelling operates as a B&B

Todhead Lighthouse, Aberdeenshire

Todhead Lighthouse is located south of Stonehaven on the coastline between Kinneff and Catterline. The lighthouse was opened in 1897 after being completed under the supervision of engineer David Alan Stevenson. The lighthouse was deactivated in 2007 and the out buildings were sold into private hands. The structure is listed as an historic building.

Description: White Tower

Location: Roadside of Kinneff

Directions: From Roadside of Kinneff, head southeast on unnamed road for 0.6 mi and turn left on unnamed road for 0.3 mi to find the lighthouse

Coordinates: 56°53'02.0"N 2°12'55.0"W

Opened: 1897

Automated: 1988

Deactivated: 2007

Height: 13 meters, 41 feet

Focal Height: 41 meters, 135 feet

Signal: 3 white flashes for every 30 seconds

Foghorn signal: N/A

Visitor Access: Grounds open, tower closed

Bell Rock Lighthouse, Angus

The Bell Rock Lighthouse is the world's oldest surviving sea-washed lighthouse. It was built by Robert Stevenson on the Bell Rock and opened in 1810. Bell Rock has been the cause of many marine disasters as it below the surface of the water except for a few hours at low tide. It was calculated that an average of six ships were lost there each year. In 1804 the loss of the HMS York with all hands was a large impetus is deciding to construct the lighthouse despite the cost due to difficult building conditions.

Description: White tower

Location: 11 miles out to sea from Arbroath

Directions: Accessible by boat

Coordinates: 56°25'58.0"N 2°23'17.0"W

Opened: 1810

Automated: 1988

Deactivated: Active

Height: 36 meters, 118 feet

Focal Height: 28 meters, 92 feet

Signal: white flash every 5 seconds

Foghorn signal: Discontinued (Was 1 blast every 60 seconds)

Visitor Access: Closed

Scurdie Ness Lighthouse, Angus

In 1867 the community of Ferryden made a request to the Commissioners of Northern Lighthouses for a lighthouse to be erected at Montrose Point. The Scurdie Ness Lighthouse was built by David and Thomas Stevenson and opened in 1870. The light was originally fixed but was changed to a flashing signal in 1907. It was automated in 1987.

Description: White tower

Location: Montrose Point

Directions: From Ferryden, head east on Brownlow Pl for 0.1 mi and turn right onto Rossie Terrace and continue onto Beacon Terrace for 1.0 mi and the site. You will need to walk part of the way.

Coordinates: 56°42'06.0"N 2°26'14.0"W

Opened: 1870

Automated: 1987

Deactivated: Active

Height: 39 meters, 128 feet

Focal Height: 34 meters, 112 feet

Signal: 3 white flashes every 20 seconds

Foghorn signal: N/A

Visitor Access: Grounds only

Rubha nan Gall Lighthouse, Argyll and Bute

The Rubha nan Gall lighthouse was built in 1857 by David and Thomas Stevenson and is operated by the Northern Lighthouse Board. The lighthouse was automated in 1960. In 2013, the former keepers' cottages were sold. One is a private home and the other is a self-catering rental.

Description: White cylindrical tower

Location: Isle of Mull

Directions: From Tobermory take the coastal trail north from the entrance near the ferry dock for 1.2 miles

Coordinates: 56°38'19.0"N 6°03'58.0"W

Opened: 1857

Automated: 1960

Deactivated: Active

Height: 19 meters, 62 feet

Focal Height: 17 meters 56 feet

Signal: White flash every 3 seconds

Foghorn signal: N/A

Visitor Access: Grounds open, tower closed

Toward Point Lighthouse, Argyll and Bute

Robert Stevenson designed Toward Point Lighthouse on the Cowal Peninsula, Firth of Clyde and the station opened in 1812. Its light guides vessels travelling between the Isle of Bute and mainland Scotland. The light was automated in 1974 and is still active. The keeper's dwellings have been sold into private ownership.

Description: White circular tower

Location: Toward Point

Directions: From the village of Toward, go south on an unnamed road for 0.2 miles

Coordinates: 55°51'44.0"N 4°58'47.0"W

Opened: 1812

Automated: 1974

Deactivated: Active

Height: 19 meters, 62 feet

Focal Height: 21 meters, 69 feet

Signal: White flash every 10 seconds

Foghorn signal: Deactivated in the 1990s, was 3 second blast every 20 seconds

Visitor Access: Closed

Carraig Fhada Lighthouse, Argyll and Bute

Carraig Fhada Lighthouse was built in 1832 by the Laird of Islay, Walter Frederick Campbell, in memory of his wife. The unusual square design was built by the David Hamilton and Son firm. There is no lantern, just a signal light shines from a mast on top of the tower

Description: Square white tower

Location: Isle of Islay

Directions: Accessible by boat

Coordinates: 55°37'12.8"N 6°12'41.7"W

Opened: 1873

Automated: 1873

Deactivated: Active

Height: 17 meters, 58 feet

Focal Height: 20 meters, 66 feet

Signal: Flashing white/red/green every 6 seconds

Foghorn signal: N/A

Visitor Access: Grounds open

Davaar Lighthouse, Argyll and Bute

The Davaar Lighthouse was built by John Barr & Co in 1854. It was designed by the engineers David and Thomas Stevenson. The original light used a mercury vapour lamp with mirrors driven by clockwork machinery. The station also had a siren fog horn signal. The light was automated in 1983.

Description: White tower

Location: Davaar Island

Directions: Tidal island linked to mainland by causeway at low tide

Coordinates: 55°25'41.0"N 5°32'26.0"W

Opened: 1854

Automated: 1983

Deactivated: Active

Height: 20 meters, 66 feet

Focal Height: 37 meters, 121 feet

Signal: 2 white flashes every 10 seconds

Foghorn signal: 2 blasts every 20 seconds

Visitor Access: Tower closed

Dubh Artach Lighthouse, Argyll and Bute

The Dubh Artach Lighthouse is built on Dhu Heartach, a remote skerry of basalt rock off the west coast of Scotland. Between 1800 and 1854 thirty vessels were wrecked on this reef and pressure grew to establish a lighthouse at the location. Due to the remoteness of the site and difficult weather conditions, the light was projected to need a large budget which was finally approved in 1865. David and Thomas Stevenson designed the lighthouse which opened in 1872.

Description: Gray granite tower, red band

Location: Dhu Heartach skerry

Directions: Accessible by boat

Coordinates: 56°07'59.0"N 6°37'58.0"W

Opened: 1872

Automated: 1971

Deactivated: Active

Height: 38 meters, 125 feet

Focal Height: 44 meters, 144 meters

Signal: 2 white flashes every 30 seconds

Foghorn signal: Discontinued (was one blast every 45 seconds)

Visitor Access: Closed

Lismore Lighthouse, Argyll and Bute

Robert Stevenson was the engineer who designed the Lismore Lighthouse. James Smith was the contractor who completed the station in 1833. It lies on a rocky inlet on the island of Eilean Musdile. It was built to aid navigation from the Firth of Lorn to Loch Linnhe to the north and also to the Sound of Mull to the west.

Description: White tower

Location: Eilean Musdile

Directions: Accessible by boat

Coordinates: 56°27'20.0"N 5°36'27.0"W

Opened: 1833

Automated: 1965

Deactivated: Active

Height: 26 meters, 85 feet

Focal Height: 31 meters, 102 feet

Signal: White flash every 10 seconds

Foghorn signal: N/A

Visitor Access: Grounds only

Loch Indaal Lighthouse, Argyll and Bute

Loch Indaal is an inland sea on the island of Islay. Loch Indaal Lighthouse is also known as Rubh'an Duin. The lighthouse is located on the southeast side of the Rhinns of Islay off Scotland's southwest coast. As the lighthouse is located near the town of Port Charlotte, it is often referred to as the Port Charlotte light. It was built in 1859 to a design of David Lillie Stevenson and Thomas Steven. The site is also known as Rubh' an Duin Light and Port Charlotte Light.

Description: White tower

Location: Isle of Islay

Directions: From Port Charlotte, head northwest on Main St/A847 for 0.3 miles and the lighthouse is on your right.

Coordinates: 55°44'41.2"N 6°22'20.1"W

Opened: 1869

Automated: 1980s

Deactivated: Active

Height: 13 meters, 43

Focal Height: 15 meters, 49 feet

Signal: 2 white/red flash every 7 seconds

Foghorn signal: N/A

Visitor Access: Grounds open, tower closed

McArthur's Head lighthouse, Argyll and Bute

McArthur's Head lighthouse is situated at the entrance to the Sound of Islay on a high cliff. It was built by David and Thomas Stevenson and opened in 1861. The lighthouse was automated in 1969 and in 2005 it was converted to a solar powered electric lamp. It is still active.

Description: White tower

Location: Isle of Islay

Directions: Accessible by boat

Coordinates: 55°45'49.9"N 6°02'51.9"W

Opened: 1861

Automated: 1969

Deactivated: Active

Height: 13 meters, 43 feet

Focal Height: 39 meters, 128 feet

Signal: 2 white flashes every 10 seconds

Foghorn signal: N/A

Visitor Access: closed

Mull of Kintyre Lighthouse, Argyll and Bute

The Mull of Kintyre lighthouse, opened in 1788, was one of the first to be erected in Scotland. The work was contracted by Peter Stuart and the job supervised by Thomas Smith. He was assisted by his son-in-law, Robert Stevenson, one of the lighthouse building family of Stevensons. In the 1820s the tower was rebuilt and in 1876 it was equipped with a fog horn. In 1906 the fixed light was changed to a flashing light.

Description: White tower on white building

Location: Southern tip of Kintyre Peninsula

Directions: From the town of Campbeltown, head west on an unnamed road for 1.6 miles and turn right on an unnamed road and go 7 miles to the lighthouse

Coordinates: 55°18'38.0"N 5°48'12.0"W

Opened: 1788

Automated: 1996

Deactivated: Active

Height: 12 meters,

Focal Height: 91 meters,

Signal: 2 white flashes every 20 seconds

Foghorn signal: The electric fog signal is 1km from the lighthouse

Visitor Access: Closed

Rinns of Islay Lighthouse, Argyll and Bute

Rhinns of Islay Lighthouse opened in 1825 and was engineered by Robert Stevenson. John Gibb of Aberdeen was the contractor. The light is situated on the small Island of Orsay off the south coast of Islay. The lighthouse was automated on 31 March 1998. The area where the lighthouse is located is a special protection zone due to its importance for breeding and wintering birds.

Description: White tower

Location: Small Island of Orsay

Directions: Accessible by boat

Coordinates: 55°40'23.0"N 6°30'48.0"W

Opened: 1825

Automated: 1998

Deactivated: Active

Height: 29 meters, 95 feet

Focal Height: 46 meters, 150 feet

Signal: White flash every 5 seconds

Foghorn signal: Discontinued (was 3 blasts every 90 seconds)

Visitor Access: Closed

Sanda Island Lighthouse, Argyll and Bute

Sanda Lighthouse was built in 1850 to plans by the engineer Alan Stevenson. The lighthouse is a complex that includes a light tower on top of Ship Rock and a two-stage stair tower linking the lighthouse with the pier and other buildings below Ship Rock. There had been calls for a lighthouse since at least 1825 when the ship Christiana was wrecked nearby with all hands lost.

Description: Masonry tower

Location: Sanda Island

Directions: Accessible by boat

Coordinates: 55°16'29.0"N 5°34'58.0"W

Opened: 1850

Automated: 1977

Deactivated: Active

Height: 15 meters, 49 feet

Focal Height: 50 meters, 160 feet

Signal: White flash every 10 seconds

Foghorn signal: Discontinued 1990 (was 1 blast every 60 seconds)

Visitor Access: Grounds open, tower closed

Scarinish Lighthouse, Argyll and Bute

Scarinish Lighthouse is located on the Isle of Tiree, the westernmost island of the Inner Hebrides. It is administered by Argyll and Bute. The lighthouse is situated on the southeast coast of the island. The original lighthouse was built by David and Thomas Stevenson which opened in 1872. The present light was more recent but the date is not available.

Description: Square tower

Location: Isle of Tiree

Directions: Accessible by boat

Coordinates: 56°30'01.0"N 6°48'15.0"W

Opened: 1872

Automated: Not known

Deactivated: Active

Height: 3.5 meters, 11 feet

Focal Height: 11 meters, 36 meters

Signal: White flash every 3 seconds

Foghorn signal: N/A

Visitor Access: Grounds open

Skerryvore Lighthouse, Argyll and Bute

Skerryvore is a cluster of rocks forming reef some 20 km west-south-west of the island of Tiree of the Inner Hebrides. Many vessels have been wrecked on this reef, with at least 26 were lost between 1790 and 1844. The lighthouse was built in 1844 by Alan Stevenson on this rock outcrop and it stands 48 meters or 156 feet tall, making it the tallest lighthouse in the UK. He designed the curve in the tower wall for its beauty as well as being a lower center of gravity. It asserted by some that Skerryvore is the world's most graceful lighthouse.

Description: Grey granite tower

Location: Skerryvore Rock

Directions: Accessible by boat

Coordinates: 56°19'23.0"N 7°06'58.0"W

Opened: 1844

Automated: 1994

Deactivated: Active

Height: 48 meters 157 feet

Focal Height: 46 meters, 151 feet

Signal: White flash every 10 seconds

Foghorn signal: Discontinued October 04, 2005

Visitor Access: Closed

Ruvaal Lighthouse, Argyll and Bute, Killarow and Kilmeny

Requests for a light at the northwest tip of Islay Island were made as early as 1835 as needed to cover the Neva Rocks. It was designed by David and Thomas Stevenson and completed in 1859. It was initially a fixed light but changed to flashing later. When the station was automated in 1982, the Dwellings were sold and are now private property.

Description: White cylindrical tower

Location: Isle of Islay

Directions: Accessible by boat

Coordinates: 55°56'11.0"N 6°07'25.0"W

Opened: 1859

Automated: 1983

Deactivated: Active

Height: 34 meters, 112 feet

Focal Height: 45 meters, 148 feet

Signal: 3 white flashes every 15 seconds

Foghorn signal: N/A

Visitor Access: Closed

Mull of Galloway Lighthouse, Dumfries and Galloway

The Mull of Galloway Lighthouse is located at the Rhins of Galloway peninsula, the southernmost point of Scotland. It is an area of natural habitat and now a protected nature preserve. The lighthouse was built by Robert Stevenson and opened in 1830. It was automated in 1988 and is still active.

Description: White tower

Location: Rhins of Galloway peninsula

Directions: 2.2 miles south of Cairngaan

Coordinates: 54°38'06.0"N 4°51'26.0"W

Opened: 1830

Automated: 1988

Deactivated: Active

Height: 26 meters, 85 feet

Focal Height: 99 meters, 325 feet

Signal: White flash every 20 seconds

Foghorn signal: Discontinued in 1987 (Was 2 blasts every 60 seconds)

Visitor Access: The lighthouse tower is open weekends from Easter to October

Corsewall Lighthouse, Dumfries and Galloway

Requests for a lighthouse on Corsewell were made in 1814 and in 1815 it was approved. It was intended to mark the east side of the channel between the Rhinns of Galloway and the Irish coast. The Corsewell Lighthouse was designed by Robert Stevenson and opened in 1817. Shortly after opening the keeper was demoted after falling asleep and leaving the light out. The site was updated by David Stevenson in 1891.

Description: White tower

Location: Corsewall Point

Directions: From Stranraer, head northeast on unnamed road for 0.1 mi and turn left for 0.3 mi. Keep left on unnamed road for 0.3 mi to find the site

Coordinates: 55°00'25.0"N 5°09'33.0"W

Opened: 1816

Automated: 1994

Deactivated: Active

Height: 34 meters, 112 feet

Focal Height: 34 meters, 112 feet

Signal: 5 white flashes every 30 seconds

Foghorn signal: Discontinued 1987 (Was 4 blasts every 90 seconds)

Visitor Access: Closed

Crammag Head Lighthouse, Dumfries and Galloway

Crammag Head Lighthouse is situated south of Stranraer, near to the Mull of Galloway. The original lighthouse at Crammag Head opened 1913. The new lighthouse became operational in December 2009. The light tower is 7 metres high and the light has an elevation of 35 metres and a range of 18 miles.

Description: White tower

Location: West of Damnaglaur

Directions: From Damnaglaur, head west for 1.5 mi and turn right on unnamed road. After 1.1 mi turn left on unnamed and park in 0.3 mi. Walk west towards the coast and the light is 0.2 mi.

Coordinates: 54°39'53.0"N 4°57'54.0"W

Opened: 2009

Automated: 2009

Deactivated: Active

Height: 7 meters, 23 feet

Focal Height: 35 meters, 115 feet

Signal: White flash every 10 seconds

Foghorn signal: N/A

Visitor Access: Closed

Killantringan Lighthouse, Dumfries and Galloway

Plans for the Killantringan Lighthouse on Black Head were finalized in 1987 and John Adams & Co of Glasgow completed the contract in 1900. The design was by engineer David Stevenson. Shortly after a fishing boat and crew were in distress and were saved by the keeper. It was the first of many successful operations. The lighthouse was automated in 1988 and became inactive in 2007.

Description: White tower

Location: Black Head

Directions: From Portslogan, head south on B738 for 1.2 mi and turn right on an unnamed road and drive 1.3 mi. Turn left on unnamed road and the light is 0.2 mi

Coordinates: 54°51'42.0"N 5°08'49.0"W

Opened: 1900

Automated: 1988

Deactivated: 2007

Height: 22 meters, 72 feet

Focal Height: 49 meters, 161 feet

Signal: 2 white flashes every 15 seconds

Foghorn signal: Discontinued 1987 (Was 3 blasts every 90 seconds)

Visitor Access: Closed

Little Ross Lighthouse, Dumfries and Galloway

Little Ross Lighthouse was one of Robert Stevenson's last lighthouse designs. The contract was completed by Robert Hume in 1843. The island lies around a quarter of a mile from the western entrance of the River Dee in Kirkcudbright Bay. The structure was built on the summit of Little Ross Island, 123 feet above sea level. Lighthouse keeper Hugh Clark was found dead on the island after he was murdered by his assistant Robert Dickson. Dickson was sentenced to death but he was reprieved shortly before his execution.

Description: White circular tower

Location: Little Ross Island

Directions: Accessible by boat

Coordinates: 54°45'57.0"N 4°05'06.0"W

Opened: 1843

Automated: 1961

Deactivated: Active

Height: 22 meters, 72 feet

Focal Height: 50 meters, 160 feet

Signal: 2 white flashes every 5 seconds

Foghorn signal: N/A

Visitor Access: Closed

Southerness Lighthouse, Dumfries and Galloway

Southerness lighthouse is located at the village of Southerness in southwest Scotland. It was built in 1748 and is the second oldest in Scotland. It was built to aid ships passing through the Solway Firth towards the Nith Estuary. It was originally a landmark for ships and was not lit until about 1800. In 1805 it was upgraded under the direction of Robert Stevenson. It has been raised twice, in 1795 and 1844.

Description: Square tower

Location: Southerness Point

Directions: South end of town of Southerness

Coordinates: 54°52'22.0"N 3°35'43.0"W

Opened: 1749

Automated: Not known

Deactivated: 1931

Height: 17 meters, 56 feet

Focal Height: 17 meters, 56 feet

Signal: Fixed light

Foghorn signal: N/A

Visitor Access: Open

Barns Ness Lighthouse, East Lothian

The Barns Ness Lighthouse was built to mark the entrance to the Firth of Forth and Edinburgh. It was constructed by the engineers and brothers David Stevenson and Charles Stevenson and opened in 1901. The lighthouse is easily accessible by road. The dwellings and other buildings were sold after the light was deactivated in 2005.

Description: White tower

Location: Dunbar

Directions: From Dunbar, head north off A1087 on an unnamed road for 1.0 miles and turn right on an unnamed road where the light is 0.9 miles

Coordinates: 55°59'14.0"N 2°26'43.0"W

Opened: 1901

Automated: 1986

Deactivated: 2005

Height: 37 meters, 121 feet

Focal Height: 36 meters, 118 feet

Signal: Discontinued 2005 (Was white flash every 4 seconds)

Foghorn signal: Discontinued 2001 (Was 1 blasts in 90 secs.)

Visitor Access: Grounds and tower closed

Bass Rock Lighthouse, East Lothian

Bass Rock Lighthouse was built in 1902 as an aid to navigation for the passage between the island and North Berwick. It was built under the supervision of David Stevenson who designed the structure. A foghorn was installed on the northeast headland in 1907 with a footpath to the lighthouse. Between 1672 and 1688 the site was a prison for Presbyterian ministers and about 40 religious prisoners died in the dungeons of the rock.

Description: White stone tower

Location: Bass Rock

Directions: Accessible by boat

Coordinates: 56°04'36.0"N 2°38'28.0"W

Opened: 1902

Automated: 1988

Deactivated: Active

Height: 20 meters, 66 feet

Focal Height: 46 meters, 151 feet

Signal: 3 white flashes every 20 seconds

Foghorn signal: Discontinued 1988 (Was 3 blasts every 120 seconds)

Visitor Access: Closed

Fidra Lighthouse, East Lothian

The lighthouse on Fidra was built by Thomas and David Stevenson and opened in 1885. It was manned until 1970 when it was the first Scottish lighthouse automated. The island is a Royal Society for the Protection of Birds (RSPB) nature reserve.

Description: White tower

Location: Fidra Island

Directions: Accessible by goat

Coordinates: 56°04'24.0"N 2°47'06.0"W

Opened: 1885

Automated: 1970

Deactivated: Active

Height: 17 meters, 56 feet

Focal Height: 34 meters, 112 feet

Signal: 4 white flashes every 30 seconds

Foghorn signal: N/A

Visitor Access: Closed

Elie Ness Lighthouse, Fife

The Elie Ness Lighthouse is situated on a peninsula jutting into the Firth of Forth. David Stevenson supervised the build and it opened in 1908 to guide ships from the cliffs between Inchkeith and the Isle of May. James Lawrie Builders was the contractor. The structure was rehabilitated in 2010 including painting the exterior. It is still active.

Description: White tower

Location: Mainland

Directions: Take the Fife Coastal Path from the southern part of Elie

Coordinates: 56°11'02.0"N 2°48'46.0"W

Opened: 1908

Automated: 1964

Deactivated: Active

Height: 11 meters, 36 feet

Focal Height: 15 meters, 49 feet

Signal: White flash every 6 seconds

Foghorn signal: N/A

Visitor Access: Grounds open, tower closed

Old Isle of May Lighthouse (The Beacon), Fife

Old Isle of May Lighthouse, commonly known as the Beacon was built in 1836 and was the first permanently manned lighthouse in Scotland. It was a stone fire beacon with a coal-burning basket on the top of the building. Tragedy struck the station in 1791 when the Keeper, his wife and 5 of 6 children died from fumes from the ash heap. The structure was privately owned and ships paid a toll to use the light. The Isle of May is a National Nature Reserve.

Description: Square white building

Location: Isle of May

Directions: Accessible by ferry from Anstruther, Crail, or North Berwick

Coordinates: 56°11'09.0"N 2°33'24.0"W

Opened: 1636

Automated: N/A

Deactivated: Not known

Height: 12 meters, 39 feet

Signal: Flame from basket of burning coal

Foghorn signal: N/A

Visitor Access: Grounds open outside of Nature Preserve restrictions

Oxcars Lighthouse, Fife

The Oxcars Lighthouse in the Firth of Forth was needed to guide ships safely up the Forth river. he lighthouse was built in 1886 by Thomas and David Stevenson. It was the first automated lighthouse in Scotland in 1894. At high tide the rock it stands on is under water.

Description: White tower with red band

Location: Firth of Forth

Directions: Accessible by boat

Coordinates: 56°01'21.0"N 3°16'49.0"W

Opened: 1886

Automated: 1894

Deactivated: Active

Height: 21 meters, 69 feet

Focal Height: 15 meters, 49 feet

Signal: white/red sector flash every 7 seconds

Foghorn signal: N/A

Visitor Access: Closed

Fife Ness Lighthouse, Fife

Fife Ness Lighthouse was built in 1975 by P. H. Hyslop. It was needed to aid mariners of the headland and the North Carr shoals. Before these rocks was marked, the North Carr Reef was responsible for the destruction of at least sixteen ships and many deaths between 1800 and 1809. Previously a series of light vessels had been utilized since it was too difficult to place a lighthouse directly on the rocks.

Description: White building

Location: Mainland

Directions: From Craighead, head east on unnamed road for 0.5 miles and the lighthouse

Coordinates: 56°16'44.0"N 2°35'09.0"W

Opened: 1975

Automated: 1975

Deactivated: Active

Height: 5 meters, 16 feet

Focal Height: 12 meters, 39 feet

Signal: Iso white flash 10 seconds.

Foghorn signal: N/A

Visitor Access: grounds open, building closed

Inchkeith Lighthouse, Fife

Inchkeith Lighthouse was built in 1804 by engineer Thomas Smith assisted by Robert Stevenson. Building of the lighthouse involved demolition of almost all of a fort built by the French after they captured the island from the English in 1549. A fog signal was added to the site in 1899. The lighthouse was automated in 1986. The lighthouse building is listed as a building of Architectural interest.

Description: Stone tower

Location: Inchkeith Island

Directions: Accessible by boat

Coordinates: 56°02'01.0"N 3°08'10.0"W

Opened: 1804

Automated: 1986

Deactivated: Active

Height: 22 meters, 62 feet

Focal Height: 67 meters, 2230 feet

Signal: White flash every 15 seconds

Foghorn signal: Discontinued 2004 (Was 4 blasts of 1.5 seconds every 60 seconds

Visitor Access: Grounds open, tower closed

Isle of May Lighthouse, Fife

In 1816 a new lighthouse was built by engineer Robert Stevenson in conjunction with the contractor James Maxwell. The Isle of May, located about 8 km east of Anstruther in the northern entrance to the Firth of Forth, is a bird and seal sanctuary, the Isle of May National Nature Reserve. The Lighthouse is located at the highest point of the island. In 1972 the keeper's families were moved to accommodations on shore in Granton.

Description: Quadrangular tower

Location: Isle of May

Directions: Accessible by ferry from Anstruther, Crail, or North Berwick

Coordinates: 56°11'08.0"N 2°33'27.0"W

Opened: 1816

Automated: 1989

Deactivated: Active

Height: 24 meters, 79 feet

Focal Height: 73 meters, 249 feet

Signal: 2 white flashes every 15 seconds

Foghorn signal: Discontinued in 1989 (was North: 1 blast every 7 seconds, South: 4 blasts every 150 seconds)

Visitor Access: Grounds open, tower closed

Isle of May Low Light, Fife

The Isle of May Low Light was opened in 1844, situated about 400 meters from the High Lighthouse. If if the two lights are seen exactly above each other the ship's captain could be avoid the treacherous North Carr Reef, 12 kilometres north of the Island. It was deactivated in 1887 after the North Carr lightship was operational. The tower is now used by the Isle of May Bird Observatory

Description: White tower

Location: Isle of May

Directions: Accessible by ferry from Anstruther, Crail, or North Berwick

Coordinates: 56°10'59.0"N 2°33'07.0"W

Opened: 1844

Automated: N/A

Deactivated: 1877

Height: Not available

Focal Height: Not available

Signal: Not available

Foghorn signal: N/A

Visitor Access: Open (Birdwatching tower)

Corran Point Lighthouse, Highland

Corran Point Lighthouse was built in 1860 as a project by Thomas Stevenson and David Stevenson. It is one of a series of lighthouses marking the route to the Caledonian Canal. The original lighthouse keepers' dwellings have been opened for holiday accommodation. It was automated in 1898, the first Scottish lighthouse to be done.

Description: White tower

Location: Corran Point

Directions: From the Corran Ardgour West Ferry Terminal, head southwest on the A861 for 0.1 miles and the lighthouse

Coordinates: 56°43'15.0"N 5°14'32.0"W

Opened: 1860

Automated: 1898

Deactivated: Active

Height: 13 meters, 43 feet

Focal Height: 12 meters, 39 feet

Signal: Iso.white/red/green every 4 seconds

Foghorn signal: N/A

Visitor Access: Closed

Dunnet Head Lighthouse, Highland

Dunnet Head Lighthouse is situated at the most northerly point of the Scottish mainland, 2.4 miles north of John O' Groats. Only 6.75 miles across the Pentland Firth lies the Orkney Isles. It was built in 1831 by James Smith under the supervision of engineer, Robert Stevenson. The lighthouse was automated in 1989. Dunnet Head is also a Royal Society for the Protection of Birds (RSPB) station.

Description: White tower

Location: Dunnet Head

Directions: From Brough, head north on B855 for 3.0 miles and you will find the site

Coordinates: 58°40'17.0"N 3°22'35.0"W

Opened: 1831

Automated: 1989

Deactivated: Active

Height: 20 meters, 66 feet

Focal Height: 105 meters, 344 feet

Signal: 4 white flashes every 30 seconds

Foghorn signal: Discontinued 1987 (Was 3 blasts every 90 seconds)

Visitor Access: Closed

Stroma Lighthouse, Highland

The Stroma Lighthouse was built in 1896 to a design by engineer David Stevenson as part of a large program of construction for northern Scotland. The keepers lived on the island until 1962 when the residents of Stroma left the island, at which time they moved to the mainland. In 1997 the station was automated.

Description: White circular tower

Location: Island of Stroma

Directions: From Nethertown, head north for 0.7 miles to find the lighthouse

Coordinates: 58°41'45.0"N 3°07'00.0"W

Opened: 1890

Automated: 1997

Deactivated: Active

Height: 23 meters, 75 feet

Focal Height: 32 meters, 105 feet

Signal: 2 white flashes every 20 seconds

Foghorn signal: Deactivated 2005 (Was 2 blasts every 60 seconds)

Visitor Access: Closed

Tarbat Ness Lighthouse, Highland

Tarbat Ness Lighthouse is the third tallest in Scotland after North Ronaldsay and Skerryvore. It was built by contractor James Smith under supervision of engineer Robert Stevenson and opened in in 1830. The lighthouse's white-painted tower had its two horizontal red bands added in 1915. It is still active.

Description: Circular tower with two red bands

Location: Tarbat peninsula

Directions: From Wilkhaven, head north on unnamed road for 0.3 miles and turn left on an unnamed road where the lighthouse is 0.3 miles

Coordinates: 57°51'54.0"N 3°46'36.0"W

Opened: 1830

Automated: 1985

Deactivated: Active

Height: 41 meters, 135 feet

Focal Height: 53 meters, 174 feet

Signal: 4 white flashes every 30 seconds

Foghorn signal: N/A

Visitor Access: Grounds open, tower closed

Waternish Lighthouse, Highland

The original lighthouse on Waternish Point was built by David and Charles Stevenson in 1924. The present tower was built in 1980, by engineer John Smith. It is made up of a concrete base, aluminum light room and a roof. Solar panels were installed in 2001 to power it. Some sources refer to this light as Vaternish Lighthouse.

Description: White tower

Location: Isle of Sky

Directions: Northern tip of Waterness Point

Coordinates: 57°36'29.0"N 6°38'03.0"W

Opened: 1980

Automated: 1980

Deactivated: Active

Height: 7 meters, 23 feet

Focal Height: 21 meters, 69 feet

Signal: White flash every 20 seconds

Foghorn signal: N/A

Visitor Access: Grounds open, tower closed

Ardnamurchan Lighthouse, Highland

Ardnamurchan Lighthouse opened in 1849, after being built by contractor Robert Hume to a design by engineer Allan Stevenson. The original lens at Ardnamurchan was a Fresnel lens, the most modern at that time. The dwellings are now operated as a visitor centre with a museum called the Kingdom of Light

Description: Gray granite tower

Location: Ardnamurchan Peninsula

Directions: From Grigadale, head west on unnamed road for 0.5 miles and turn left on unnamed road and see the lighthouse in 0.9 miles

Coordinates: 56°43'38.0"N 6°13'34.0"W

Opened: 1849

Automated: 1988

Deactivated: Active

Height: 36 meters, 118 feet

Focal Height: 55 meters, 180 feet

Signal: 2 white flashes every 20 seconds

Foghorn signal: Discontinued 2005 (Was 2 blasts every 20 seconds)

Visitor Access: Yes (Ardnamurchan Lighthouse Visitor Centre)

Cape Wrath Lighthouse, Highland

The Lighthouse was built of large blocks of granite by Robert Stevenson in 1828. The optics are a first order Fresnel lens. As the station is not easily reached by road, supplies were landed by ship. The lighthouse was manned until 1998, when it was converted to automatic operation.

Description: White tower

Location: Cape Wrath

Directions: Visitors can cross the Kyle of Durness by ferry and then travel twelve miles by minibus

Coordinates: 58°37'32.0"N 4°59'57.0"W

Opened: 1828

Automated: 1998

Deactivated: Active

Height: 20 meters, 66 feet

Focal Height: 122 meters, 400 feet

Signal: 4 white flashes every 30 seconds

Foghorn signal: Discontinued 2001 (Was 1 blast every 90 seconds)

Visitor Access: Guided tours are available from Durness

Cromarty Lighthouse, Highland

In 1842, the Board of Trade commissioned a lighthouse to be built in the village of Cromarty. This lighthouse was to guide vessels from the North Sea to the Moray Firth and the Cromarty Firth. David Mitchell was the contractor for a design by Allan Stevenson and the light opened in 1846. In 1985 the lighthouse was automated and in 2005 it became inactive. The University of Aberdeen now owns the buildings.

Description: Circular white tower

Location: Town of Cromarty

Directions: In Cromarty, the lighthouse is on George Street off Bank Street

Coordinates: 57°40'59.0"N 4°02'11.0"W

Opened: 1846

Automated: 1985

Deactivated: 2006

Height: 13 meters, 43 feet

Focal Height: 18 meters, 59 feet

Signal: Occulting White and Red every 10 seconds

Foghorn signal: N/A

Visitor Access: Yes

Duncansby Head Lighthouse, Highland

Duncansby Head is the most north-easterly part of the Scottish mainland. Duncansby Head Lighthouse was built in 1924 by David Alan Stevenson. It originally was lit by a Fourth order Fresnel lens. The station was automated in 1997. The keeper's houses showed asbestos on the premises and were demolished.

Description: White tower

Location: Duncansby Head

Directions: A minor public road leads from John o' Groats to Duncansby Head

Coordinates: 58°38'38.0"N 3°01'31.0"W

Opened: 1924

Automated: 1997

Deactivated: Active

Height: 11 meters, 36 feet

Focal Height: 67 meters, 220 feet

Signal: White flash every 12 seconds

Foghorn signal: Discontinued 1987 (Was 5 blasts every 120 sec)

Visitor Access: No

Hyskeir Lighthouse, Highland

Haskeir is a remote, uninhabited island in the Outer Hebrides. The Hyskeir Lighthouse was established in 1904. It was designed by David and Charles Stevenson and constructed by Oban contractor D & J MacDougall and warns of the Mills Rocks, Canna, and Hyskeir. The tower was manned until March 1997, before becoming one of the last lighthouses in Scotland to be automated.

Description: White tower

Location: Hyskeir island

Directions: Accessible by boat

Coordinates: 56°58'08.0"N 6°40'51.0"W

Opened: 1904

Automated: 1997

Deactivated: Active

Height: 39 meters, 128 feet

Focal Height: 41 meters, 135 feet

Signal: 3 white flashes every 30 seconds

Foghorn signal: N/A

Visitor Access: Closed

Neist Point Lighthouse, Highland

Neist Point Lighthouse was designed by David Alan Stevenson and built by W. Hugh MacDonald. It was first lit in 1909. An aerial cableway was used to take supplies to the lighthouse and cottages. The site was automated in 1990 and the former keepers' cottages are now in private ownership.

Description: Circular white tower

Location: Neist Point

Directions: On the Isle of Skye, head south from Waterstein for 0.6 miles on an unnamed road and walk south from parking area

Coordinates: 57°25'24.0"N 6°47'18.0"W

Opened: 1909

Automated: 1990

Deactivated: Active

Height: 19 meters, 62 feet

Focal Height: 43 meters, 141 feet

Signal: White flash every 5 seconds

Foghorn signal: Discontinued 2005 (Was 2 blasts every 90 seconds)

Visitor Access: Closed

Noss Head Lighthouse, Highland

The Noss Head Lighthouse was built by contractor Mr. Arnot under the supervision of engineer Alan Stevenson. The light opened in 1849. A new style of lantern with diagonal instead of vertical framing was developed by Stevenson and first used at Noss Head. The light was automated in 1987 and the dwellings were sold into private hands at that time.

Description: White tower

Location: Noss Head

Directions: From Wick, head NW on Broadhaven Rd for 0.6 mi. Continue onto Elzy Rd for 0.1 mi. Turn left on unnamed road and drive 0.9 mi. Turn right and the site is 1.8 mi

Coordinates: 58°28'44.0"N 3°03'03.0"W

Opened: 1849

Automated: 1957

Deactivated: Active

Height: 18 meters, 59 feet

Focal Height: 53 meters, 174 feet

Signal: White flash every 20 seconds

Foghorn signal: Discontinued 1985 (Was 3 blasts every 90 seconds)

Visitor Access: Closed

Ornsay Lighthouse, Highlands

Ornsay Lighthouse was built by David and Thomas Stevenson and opened in 1857. The station was automated in 1962 and in 1966 the dwellings were sold into private hands. The light was modernized in 1988 when electric power was installed to replace the gas system. It remains active today.

Description: White tower

Location: Off Ornsay Island

Directions: Accessible by boat

Coordinates: 57°08'36.0"N 5°46'52.0"W

Opened: 1857

Automated: 1962

Deactivated: Active

Height: 19 meters, 62 feet

Focal Height: 18 meters, 59 feet

Signal: Occulting White every 8 seconds

Foghorn signal: N/A

Visitor Access: Closed

Point of Sleat Lighthouse, Highland

The Point of Sleat Lighthouse is a lighthouse in the Inner Hebrides on the Isle of Skye. The original lighthouse was built in 1934 at the Point of Sleat at the southern end of the island. In 2003 the tower was demolished and replaced by a square concrete structure with a solar powered light

Description: White tower

Location: Isle of Skye

Directions: Accessible by boat or long coastal walk

Coordinates: 57°01'06.0"N 6°01'03.0"W

Opened: 2003

Automated: 2003

Deactivated: Active

Height: 5 meters, 16 feet

Focal Height: 20 meters, 66 feet

Signal: White flash every 3 seconds

Foghorn signal: N/A

Visitor Access: Grounds open

Rona Lighthouse, Highland

Rona Lighthouse is a lighthouse in South Rona, off the isle of Skye. The lighthouse was built to the design of engineers Thomas Stevenson and David Stevenson and was completed in 1857. By the 1930s the keepers were the only people on the island as all the other residents had relocated. The lighthouse was automated in 1975.

Description: White tower

Location: South Rona

Directions: Accessible by boat

Coordinates: 57°34'41.0"N 5°57'33.0"W

Opened: 1857

Automated: 1975

Deactivated: Active

Height: 13 meters, 43 feet

Focal Height: 69 meters, 226 feet

Signal: White flash every 12 seconds

Foghorn signal: N/A

Visitor Access: Open

Rua Reidh Lighthouse, Highland

Rua Reidh Lighthouse stands close to the entrance to Loch Ewe in Wester Ross, Scotland. David Stevenson proposed building a lighthouse there in 1853 but one was not built until 1912 when his son, David Alan Stevenson oversaw its erection. It was originally equipped with a state of the art Fresnel lens which is now in the Gairloch Heritage Museum. The fog signal was discontinued in 1980.

Description: White tower

Location: Entrance to Loch Ewe

Directions: From Melvaig, head NW on B8021 for 3.5 mi to find the station

Coordinates: 57°51'32.0"N 5°48'43.0"W

Opened: 1912

Automated: 1986

Deactivated: Active

Height: 25 meters, 82 feet

Focal Height: 37 meters, 121 feet

Signal: 4 white flashed every 15 seconds

Foghorn signal: Discontinued 1980 (Was 4 blasts every 90 seconds)

Visitor Access: Grounds open

Stoer Head Lighthouse, Highland

Stoer Head Lighthouse was built by brothers David and Thomas Stevenson in 1870. About 10,000 visitors visit the lighthouse yearly and there is parking and toilets available. For many years sea transport was the only way of delivering supplies to the station and a jetty was built for this. The lighthouse was automated in 1978.

Description: White tower

Location: Stoer Head

Directions: From Raffin, head west on unnamed road for 1.2 miles

Coordinates: 58°14'24.0"N 5°24'09.0"W

Opened: 1870

Automated: 1978

Deactivated: Active

Height: 14 meters, 46 feet

Focal Height: 59 meters, 194 feet

Signal: White flash every 15 seconds

Foghorn signal: Discontinued

Visitor Access: Open

Strathy Point Lighthouse, Highland

Strathy Point Lighthouse was the last lighthouse to be built, in 1958, that was intended for manned operation. All later lights were intended for automated operation from inception. The station was initially equipped with a 4th order optic which was changed to a solar powered LED when the light was automated in 1997.

Description: White tower on building

Location: Strathy Point

Directions: From Thurso, head north on an unnamed road for 2.6 miles

Coordinates: 58°35'55.0"N 4°01'07.0"W

Opened: 1958

Automated: 1997

Deactivated: 2012

Height: 14 meters, 46 feet

Focal Height: 45 meters, 148 feet

Signal: White flash every 20 seconds

Foghorn signal: Discontinued 1987 (Was 4 blasts every 90 seconds)

Visitor Access: Grounds open, buildings closed

Chanonry Lighthouse, Highland and Fortrose

The establishment of a lighthouse on Chanonry Point was proposed in 1834 and in 1837 by the Commissioners' Engineer, Alan Stevenson but it was not approved until 1843. Alan Stevenson supervised the work and the lighthouse opened in 1846. Chanonry Lighthouse lies at the end of a spit of land stretching into the Moray Firth between Fortrose and Rosemarkie Bay on the Black Isle. The site was automated in 1984.

Description: White tower

Location: Chanonry Point

Directions: From Fortrose, head east on Ness Rd for 1.3 mi to find the site

Coordinates: 57°34'26.0"N 4°05'34.0"W

Opened: 1846

Automated: 1984

Deactivated: Active

Height: 13 meters, 43 feet

Focal Height: 12 meters, 39 feet

Signal: Occulting White every 6 Seconds

Foghorn signal: Discontinued 2001 (Was 6 blasts in 90 seconds)

Visitor Access: Closed

Cloch Lighthouse, Inverclyde

The Cloch is one of the three lighthouses built to protect shipping at the head of the Firth of Clyde, the other two being on Little Cumbrae and Toward Point. The station was designed and built by Thomas Smith and Robert Stevenson and opened in 1797. The three keeper's dwellings were sold in 1986. The light is fully automated and unmanned. The main light has been replaced by a light on a pole outside the lantern room.

Description: White tower with black band

Location: Cloch Point

Directions: From Ardgowan, head northwest on A770 to find the light

Coordinates: 55°56'32.0"N 4°52'43.0"W

Opened: 1797

Automated: 1974

Deactivated: Active

Height: 23 meters, 76 feet

Focal Height: 23 meters, 76 feet

Signal: White flash every 3 seconds

Foghorn signal: Deactivated

Visitor Access: Closed

Covesea Skerries Lighthouse, Moray, Lossiemouth and Branderburgh

Covesea Skerries Lighthouse had been called for since 1826 when 16 ships sank in the Moray Firth in a storm. It was not built until 1846 when the contractor was James Smith and a design by Alan Stevenson. The station was originally equipped with a Fresnel lens. The dwellings are available for holiday rental.

Description: White tower

Location: Covesea Skerries

Directions: From Covesea, head east on B9040 for 1.1 mi and turn left on an unnamed road to find the site in 0.3 mi

Coordinates: 57°43'27.0"N 3°20'19.0"W

Opened: 1846

Automated: 1984

Deactivated: 2012

Height: 36 meters, 118 feet

Focal Height: 49 meters, 161 feet

Signal: White/red flash every 20 seconds

Foghorn signal: N/A

Visitor Access: Grounds open, tower closed

Little Cumbrae Old Lighthouse, North Ayrshire

A lighthouse on Little Cumbrae Island was needed to guide ships through the Firth of Clyde. James Ewing completed the original tower in 1757 with a coal fire providing the light. It was discontinued in 1793 and replaced as it was often hidden by fog due to its placement and inadequacy of the light source. The original tower still stands. In 1956 the Clyde Port Authority carried out restoration work on it.

Description: Stone tower

Location: Little Cumbrae Island

Directions: Accessible by boat

Coordinates: 55°43'15.0"N 4°57'29.0"W

Opened: 1757

Automated: Never

Deactivated: 1997

Height: 8.5 meters, 28 feet

Focal Height: 18 meters, 59 feet

Signal: Coal fire

Foghorn signal: N/A

Visitor Access: Open

Cumbrae Lighthouse, North Ayrshire

The Cumbrae Lighthouse was designed and built in 1793 by Thomas Smith as an aid to ships travelling through the Firth of Clyde. It replaced the coal fire beacon lit in 1757. It had a foghorn, slipway, jetty, and boathouse. In 1865, the first foghorn in Britain was installed. The tower underwent a restoration in 1956. It was deactivated in 1997.

Description: Hexagonal cylindrical tower

Location: Little Cumbrae Island

Directions: Accessible by boat

Coordinates: 55°43'16.0"N 4°58'01.0"W

Opened: 1793

Automated: Never

Deactivated: 1997

Height: 8.5 meters, 28 feet

Focal Height: 18 meters, 59 feet

Signal: White flash every 6 seconds

Foghorn signal: Discontinued (Was 5 blasts every 35 seconds)

Visitor Access: Grounds open, tower closed

Little Cumbrae New Lighthouse, North Ayrshire

Little Cumbrae New Lighthouse was built in 1997 to replace the old lighthouse from 1793. It has always been automated. The old keeper's dwellings and out buildings have deteriorated since then.

Description: White tower

Location: Little Cumbrae Island

Directions: Accessible by boat

Coordinates: 55°43'14.0"N 4°58'02.0"W

Opened: 1997

Automated: 1997

Deactivated: Active

Height: 6 meters, 20 feet

Focal Height: 11 meters, 33 feet

Signal: White flash every 6 seconds

Foghorn signal: N/A

Visitor Access: Grounds open, tower closed

Holy Isle Inner Lighthouse, North Ayrshire

The Holy Isle Inner Lighthouse on Holy Isle faces the east coast of the Isle of Arran at the south entrance of Lamlash Bay. The lighthouse was built in 1877 and was engineered by David and Thomas Stevenson. The island is home to a Buddhist Religious community. The lighthouse was fully automated in 1977.

Description: White tower

Location: Holy Island

Directions: Accessible by boat

Coordinates: 55°30'44.0"N 5°04'13.0"W

Opened: 1877

Automated: 1977

Deactivated: Active

Height: 14 meters, 46 feet

Focal Height: 17 meters, 56 feet

Signal: Green flash every 3 seconds

Foghorn signal: N/A

Visitor Access: Open

Holy Isle Outer Lighthouse, North Ayrshire

Holy Isle Outer Lighthouse, built in 1905 by David and Charles Stevenson, is also known as Pillar Rock. It is one of two lighthouses on Holy Island, that make up a pair, the other being the Holy Island Inner Lighthouse. It is located on the east shore at Pillar Rock Point, the south eastern point of the island. This lighthouse was the third, after the Sanda Lighthouse and Pladda Lighthouses, in a series of lights that guide ships into the Firth of Clyde.

Description: Square white tower

Location: Holy Island

Directions: Accessible by boat

Coordinates: 55°31'02.0"N 5°03'39.0"W

Opened: 1905

Automated: 1977

Deactivated: Active

Height: 23 meters, 75

Focal Height: 38 meters, 125 meters

Signal: 2 white flashed every 20 seconds

Foghorn signal: Discontinued 1987 (Was 1 Blast ever 90 seconds)

Visitor Access: Grounds open, tower closed

Pladda Lighthouse, North Ayrshire

Pladda is an uninhabited island 1 mile off the south coast of the Isle of Arran in the Firth of Clyde. The Pladda Lighthouse was built in 1790 under the supervision of Thomas Smith. It protects the entrance to the Firth of Clyde and Kilbrannan Sound. In 1876, Pladda was the third station to have a foghorn. The station was automated in 1990 and is still active.

Description: White tower

Location: Island of Pladda

Directions: Accessible by boat

Coordinates: 55°25'30.0"N 5°07'06.0"W

Opened: 1790

Automated: 1990

Deactivated: Active

Height: 29 meters, 95 feet

Focal Height: 40 meters, 130 feet

Signal: 3 white flashes every 30 seconds

Foghorn signal: Discontinued 2005 (Was 1 blast every 20 seconds)

Visitor Access: Closed

Hoy Sound High Light, Orkney

The light was built in 1851 by Alan Stevenson as was the companion, Hoy Sound Low Light. It is a cylindrical tower with balcony and white painted with black lantern and the ochre trim. It was built to mark the main channel into Scapa Flow. The island can be visited by ferry from Stromness and a 1 mile round trip walk. Hoy Sound Low Light is 1.4 miles west of it.

Description: Cylindrical tower

Location: Graemsay Island

Directions: On the north tip of Graemsay Island off of Hoy. Accessible by boat

Coordinates: 58°56'08.0"N 3°16'23.0"W

Opened: 1851

Automated: 1978

Deactivated: Active

Height: 33 meters, 108 feet

Focal Height: 35 meters, 115 feet

Signal: Occulting white and red every 8 seconds

Visitor Access: Closed

Hoy Sound Low Light, Orkney

The light was also built in 1851 by Alan Stevenson as was the companion, Hoy Sound High Light. It is a cylindrical stone tower with ochre coloured balcony and lantern It was built to mark the main channel into Scapa Flow. The island can be visited by ferry from Stromness and a 1.5 mile round trip walk. The site has a one story keepers dwelling. Hoy Sound High Light is 1.4 miles east of it.

Description: Gray tower

Location: Graemsay Island

Directions: On the north tip of Graemsay Island off of Hoy. Accessible by boat

Coordinates: 58°56'25.0"N 3°18'36.0"W

Opened: 1851

Automated: 1978

Deactivated: Active

Height: 12 meters, 39 feet

Focal Height: 17 meters, 56 feet

Signal: Iso White, 3 second period

Visitor Access: Closed

North Ronaldsay Lighthouse, Orkney

North Ronaldsay was the third lighthouse built in Scotland, preceded by Kinnaird Head and Mull of Kintyre. It was lit by the catadioptric or reflecting system, which was the most advanced at the time. At 139 feet, it is the highest land based lighthouse in the British Isles. In 1889, the red brick tower was painted with two white bands. North Ronaldsay Lighthouse was automated on 30 March 1998.

Description: Red brick tower with two white bands

Location: North Ronaldsay Island

Directions: From the ferry dock from Kirkwall, go 3.7 miles north on the unnamed road

Coordinates: 59°23'23.0"N 2°22'53.0"W

Opened: 1852

Automated: 1998

Deactivated: Active

Height: 42 meters, 138 feet

Focal Height: 43 meters, 141 feet

Signal: White flash every 10 seconds

Foghorn signal: 3 blast every 60 seconds

Visitor Access: The tower is open for tours on Sunday from May to September

Dennis Head Old Beacon Lighthouse, Orkney

Dennis Head Old Beacon is a ruined lighthouse on the island of North Ronaldsay, Orkney, Scotland. The beacon and keepers' houses are protected as a historic property. The 70-foot tower was completed in 1789 by Thomas Smith, a relative of the Stevenson family of lighthouse builders. After a Lighthouse was built at Start Point, the lighthouse was considered unnecessary and became inactive in 1809. There has been discussion about repairing the spiral staircase to allow visitors.

Description: Gray cylindrical tower

Location: North Ronaldsay Island

Directions: From the ferry dock from Kirkwall, go 3.7 miles north on the unnamed road

Coordinates: 59°23'03.0"N 2°22'17.0"W

Opened: 1789

Automated: N/A

Deactivated: 1908

Height: 21 meters, 69 feet

Focal Height: N/A

Signal: N/A

Visitor Access: Closed

Start Point Lighthouse, Orkney

The lighthouse was completed on 2 October 1806 by engineer Thomas Smith. It was equipped with a parabolic reflector and later upgraded with a Fourth Order Fresnel lens. In 1870, the tower was rebuilt. It was automated in 1962 and powered by solar panels. During the building of the structure, the workmen were returning by ship to Leith when they were hit by a heavy storm. All the men were lost except the cabin boy who was found holding tight to the mast.

Description: White round granite tower

Location: Start Island

Directions: Accessible by boat

Coordinates: 59°16'39.0"N 2°22'33.0"W

Opened: 1806

Automated: 1962

Deactivated: Active

Height: 235 meters, 92 feet

Focal Height: 62 meters, 203 feet

Signal: 3 white flashes every 30 seconds

Foghorn signal: 1 blast every 30 seconds

Visitor Access: Open to visitors on occasion

Auskerry Lighthouse, Orkney

The Auskerry Lighthouse was built to guide ships into the Stronsay Firth. It was completed by David and Thomas Stevenson in 1866. Auskerry means East Skerry in Old Norse. In 1926, the Norwegian cargo ship SS County Hastings ran aground on the island, and broke up with remains widely scattered. In July 1961 it was the first Orkney Lighthouse to be automated.

Description: White cylindrical stone tower

Location: Auskerry Island

Directions: Accessible by boat

Coordinates: 59°01'33.0"N 2°34'20.0"W

Opened: 1866

Automated: 1961

Deactivated: Active

Height: 34 meters, 112 feet

Focal Height: 34 meters, 112 feet

Signal: White flash every 20 seconds

Foghorn signal: N/A

Visitor Access: Closed

Brough of Birsay Lighthouse, Orkney

The unmanned Brough of Birsay Lighthouse was designed and built built by David A Stevenson in 1925. It is located on the uninhabited tidal island, the Brough of Birsay which is on the Orkney Mainland. The lighthouse was converted to solar power in 2002. It is a very popular spot to visit with an archaeological site worth seeing as well.

Description: White tower, black lantern, ochre trim

Location: Brough of Birsay

Directions: From Birsay you can walk to the island and lighthouse when the tide is out.

Coordinates: 59°08'13.0"N 3°20'21.0"W

Opened: 1925

Automated: 1925

Deactivated: Active

Height: 11 meters, 36 feet

Focal Height: 52 meters, 171 feet

Signal: 3 white flash every 25 seconds

Foghorn signal: N/A

Visitor Access: Closed

Cantick Head Lighthouse, Orkney

The Cantick Head Lighthouse was erected to aid mariners on the southern entrance to Scapa Flow. It was built at the end of Cantick Head, a long peninsula on the south-eastern coast of South Walls overlooking the Pentland Firth. The design and construction was by Thomas and David Stevenson. Next to the tower are a set of keeper's cottages within a walled compound containing a sundial. In 1913, a foghorn was established at the site which was in use until 1987. In 1991 the lighthouse was automated, and the keeper's houses were sold.

Description: White stone tower

Location: South Walls Island off Hoy

Directions: South Walls is joined to the larger island of Hoy by a narrow causeway

Coordinates: 58°47'14.0"N 3°07'53.0"W

Opened: 1858

Automated: 1991

Deactivated: 1987

Height: 22 meters, 72 feet

Focal Height: 35 meters, 115 feet

Signal: White flash every 20 seconds

Foghorn signal: Deactivated in 1987

Visitor Access: Tower closed, keepers dwelling available for accommodation

Copinsay Lighthouse, Orkney

The lighthouse was built by two contractors and opened in 1915. A Mr McDougall built the bottom 30 feet of the tower, while Harry Taylor finished the top. The lighting apparatus is a refractor . The foghorn was compressed air powered by diesel engines. Copinsay is an important bird sanctuary and is closed to visitors. The light was automated in 1991.

Description: White tower

Location: Copinsay Island

Directions: Grounds are closed. Can be seen from ferry

Coordinates: 58°53'47.0"N 2°40'19.0"W

Opened: 1915

Automated: 1991

Deactivated: Active

Height: 21 meters, 69 feet

Focal Height: 79 meters, 259 feet

Signal: 5 white flashes every 30 seconds

Foghorn signal: Discontinued 1985 (Was 4 blasts every 60 seconds)

Visitor Access: Nature reserve closed to visitors

Hoxa Head Lighthouse, Orkney

In 1901 a cast iron, gas-powered lighthouse was built by brothers Charles and David Stevenson to guide ships into Scapa Flow. In 1996 it was replaced by the current structure which is a square metal frame covered with glass fibre reinforced plastic. The old tower was dismantled and rebuilt at the Museum of Scottish Lighthouses in Aberdeenshire. Hoxa Head Lighthouse is operated remotely from the Northern Lighthouse Board in Edinburgh.

Description: White metal framework tower

Location: South Ronaldsay

Directions: From Hoxa on the Mainland, head west on unnamed road for 1.3 miles and turn right on unnamed road for 0.3 mi. The light is a short walk northwest near the coast

Coordinates: 58°49'19.0"N 3°02'05.0"W

Opened: 1901

Automated: 1901

Deactivated: Active

Height: 6 meters, 23 feet

Focal Height: 15 meters, 49 feet

Signal: Flashing white then red, every 3 seconds

Foghorn signal: N/A

Visitor Access: Easily viewed

Lothar Rock Lighthouse, Orkney

Lothar Rock Light is a skeleton frame light built by David Stevenson in 1910. It is automated and operated by the Northern Lighthouse Board

Description: Pyramid skeleton frame

Location: Lothar Rock off the southern tip of South Ronaldsay

Directions: The ferry to Burrick, South Ronaldsay passes nearby

Coordinates: 58°43'48.0"N 2°58'42.0"W

Opened: 1910

Automated: 1910

Deactivated: Active

Height: 12 meters, 39 feet

Focal Height: 13 meters, 43 feet

Signal: 2 white flashes

Foghorn signal: N/A

Visitor Access: Closed

Noup Head Lighthouse, Orkney

Noup Head Lighthouse is located on the north west headland of the isle of Westray, in Orkney, Scotland. It was constructed by David A Stevenson in 1898 for the Northern Lighthouse Board. A Principal Lightkeeper, an Assistant and their families, lived at Noup Head until the light was automated in 1964. It was converted to wind and solar power in 2000. There is a rough path of 2.7 miles northwest from near Noltland Castle which brings you to the site.

Description: White tower

Location: Westray Island

Directions: Rough track from Noltland Castle

Coordinates: 59°19'52.0"N 3°04'13.0"W

Opened: 1898

Automated: 1964

Deactivated: Active

Height: 24 meters, 79 feet

Focal Height: 79 meters, 259 feet

Signal: White flash every 60 seconds

Foghorn signal: N/A

Visitor Access: Closed

Pentland Skerries High Lighthouse, Orkney

The lighthouse was built in 1794 by Thomas Smith and Robert Stevenson. Initially there were two towers built with fixed lights. In 1895 the light signal was changed to flashing and the smaller tower was deactivated. The light was converted to electrical operation in 1939. The lighthouse tower is listed as a building of Historical interest.

Description: White tower

Location: Muckle Skerry

Directions: Accessible by boat

Coordinates: 58°41'25.0"N 2°55'29.0"W

Opened: 1794

Automated: 1994

Deactivated: Active

Height: 24 meters, 79 feet

Focal Height: 79 meters, 259 feet

Signal: 3 white flashes every 30 seconds

Foghorn signal: N/A

Visitor Access: Closed

Sule Skerry Lighthouse, Orkney

The Sule Skerry Lighthouse was the most remote manned lighthouse in Great Britain from its opening in 1895 till it was automated in 1982. Radio beacons were established in 1929 to aid mariners in determining their location. The station was bombed in 1942 but there was little damage

Description: White tower

Location: Sule Skerry

Directions: Accessible by boat

Coordinates: 59°05'03.0"N 4°24'24.0"W

Opened: 1895

Automated: 1982

Deactivated: Active

Height: 27 meters, 89 feet

Focal Height: 34 meters, 112 feet

Signal: 2 white flashes every 15 seconds

Foghorn signal: N/A

Visitor Access: Closed

Tor Ness Lighthouse, Orkney

The lighthouse is located at the southwestern corner of Hoy and it provides aid to mariners entering by the northwest to Pentland Firth. It can be accessed by road and then walking but is not easy to find. A hand held GPS would be helpful. This lighthouse was designed and built by brothers Charles and David Stevenson.

Description: White tower

Location: Island of Hoy

Directions: From Melsetter on Hoy, go west on an unnamed road for 0.2 miles and at roads end, walk 0.2 miles west. The lighthouse is on the coast

Coordinates: 58°46'43.0"N 3°17'47.0"W

Opened: 1980

Automated: 1980

Deactivated: Active

Height: 8 meters, 26 feet

Focal Height: 21 meters, 69 feet

Signal: White flash every 3 seconds

Foghorn signal: N/A

Visitor Access: Grounds open, tower closed

Flannan Isles Lighthouse, Outer Hebrides

The Flannan Isles Lighthouse is built on the highest point of Eilean Mòr, one of the remote Flannan Isles in the Outer Hebrides. The lighthouse was built by contractor George Lawson in 1899 under the supervision of engineer David Allan Stevenson. The location is known for the "Mystery of the Disappearing Keepers". In 1900 the three lighthouse keeper's on duty vanished and no conclusive explanation has been found. A popular theory is that the men were working outdoors and a rogue wave swept them away.

Description: White tower

Location: Eilean Mòr

Directions: Accessible by boat

Coordinates: 58°17'18.0"N 7°35'17.0"W

Opened: 1899

Automated: 1971

Deactivated: Active

Height: 23 meters, 75 feet

Focal Height: 101 meters, 331 feet

Signal: 2 white flashes every 30 seconds

Foghorn signal: N/A

Visitor Access: Closed

North Rona Lighthouse, Outer Hebrides

The North Rona Lighthouse lies on the island Rona, an uninhabited Scottish island in the North Atlantic. A new west coast tanker route from Sullom Voe oil terminal in Shetland developed in the early 1980s necessitating a major new light on North Rona. It opened in 1984 with up to date equipment. A solar array was added in 2004. The area is a nature reserve, for its important grey seal and seabird colonies.

Description: White square tower

Location: Rona Island

Directions: Accessible by boat

Coordinates: 59°07'17.0"N 5°48'53.0"W

Opened: 1984

Automated: 1984

Deactivated: Active

Height: 10 meters, 33 feet

Focal Height: 114 meters, 374 meters

Signal: 3 white flashes every 20 seconds

Foghorn signal: N/A

Visitor Access: Grounds open, tower closed

Tiumpan Head Lighthouse, Outer Hebrides

The Tiumpan Head Lighthouse was built by John Aitken and designed by David and Charles Stevenson. It opened in 1900. The lighthouse was automated in 1985 and the dwellings were sold. The site is still active.

Description: White tower

Location: Isle of Lewis

Directions: From Portvoller, head north on unnamed named road off A866 and the site is 1.0 mile

Coordinates: 58°15'40.0"N 6°08'20.0"W

Opened: 1900

Automated: 1985

Deactivated: Active

Height: 21 meters, 69 feet

Focal Height: 55 meters, 180 feet

Signal: 22 white flashes every 15 seconds

Foghorn signal: Discontinued 1984 (Was 3 blasts every 90 seconds)

Visitor Access: Closed

Barra Head Lighthouse, Outer Hebrides

Barra Head Lighthouse was designed by Robert Stevenson and built by James Smith which was completed in 1833. The tower is 693 feet above sea level, the highest in Britain. In 1980 the station was automated and the keepers were withdrawn. A Blenheim bomber crashed into the cliffs nearby during World War II, but was not found until years later by a rock climber

Description: White stone tower

Location: Barra Head

Directions: Accessible by boat

Coordinates: 56°47'07.0"N 7°39'13.0"W

Opened: 1833

Automated: 1980

Deactivated: Active

Height: 18 meters, 59 feet

Focal Height: 208 meters, 693 feet

Signal: White flash every 15 seconds

Foghorn signal: N/A

Visitor Access: Closed

Butt of Lewis Lighthouse, Outer Hebrides

The Butt of Lewis Lighthouse is on the Isle of Lewis in the Outer Hebrides. It was built by John Barr and Co in 1862 and engineered by David Stevenson. It is said to be the windiest location in the United Kingdom. The light was automated in 1998, one of the last in Scotland. It continues to be active.

Description: Red brick tower

Location: Butt of Lewis

Directions: From Port of Ness, head north on B8014 for 1.4 miles and turn right on an unnamed road and find the site in 1.1 miles

Coordinates: 58°30'56.0"N 6°15'39.0"W

Opened: 1862

Automated: 1988

Deactivated: Active

Height: 37 meters, 121 feet

Focal Height: 52 meters, 171 feet

Signal: White flash every 5 seconds

Foghorn signal: Discontinued 1995 (Was 2 blasts every 90 seconds)

Visitor Access: Grounds open, tower closed

Eilean Glas Lighthouse, Outer Hebrides

The original Eilean Glas Lighthouse was built by Thomas Smith and opened in 1789. It was replaced in 1824 by Robert Stevenson, Smith's stepson. The lightroom was raised 25 feet above ground level, bringing its height to 73 feet above sea level. The station was automated in 1978 and is still active. In 2004, the owners of the lighthouse building were convicted of running a fraudulent charity to pay for the property.

Description: White tower with red bands

Location: Scalpay Island

Directions: Accessible by boat

Coordinates: 57°51'25.0"N 6°38'31.0"W

Opened: 1824

Automated: 1978

Deactivated: Active

Height: 30 meters, 98 feet

Focal Height: 43 meters, 141 feet

Signal: 3 white flashes every 20 seconds

Foghorn signal: Discontinued 1987 (Was 1 blast of 7 seconds every 90 seconds)

Visitor Access: Closed

Monach (Old and New) Lighthouse, Outer Hebrides

The original lighthouse was built under supervision of David Lillie Stevenson and Thomas Stevenson and opened in 1864. In 1942 the light was deactivated due to wartime hostilities. After the war it was derided it was not needed and was not re-lit. The new lighthouse opened in 1997 as needed for oil tankers from Shetland but was found inadequate and deactivated in 2008 and the old lighthouse was reactivated.

Old

Description: Circular brick tower

Location: Shillay Island

Directions: Accessible by boat

Coordinates: 57°31'33.0"N 7°41'46.0"W

Opened: 1864 Reopened 2008

Automated: 2008

Deactivated: Active

Height: 41 meters, 135 feet

Focal Height: 47 meters, 154 feet

Signal: 2 White flash every 15 seconds

Foghorn signal: N/A

Visitor Access: Closed

New

Description: White fibreglass tower

Location: Shillay Island

Directions: Accessible by boat

Coordinates: 57°31'33.0"N 7°41'44.0"W

Opened: 1997

Automated: 1997

Deactivated: 2008

Height: 9 meters, 30 feet

Height: 9 meters, 30 feet

Signal: Was 2 white flash every 15 seconds

Foghorn signal: N/A

Visitor Access: Closed

Ushenish Lighthouse, Outer Hebrides

The Ushenish Lighthouse is situated on the isolated east coast of South Uist. A. MacDonald was the contractor for the station which was designed by David Lillie Stevenson and Thomas Stevenson and opened in 1857. The site was automated in 1979 and is still active. Solar panels were installed in 1998 to power the station.

Description: White tower

Location: South Uist

Directions: Accessible by boat

Coordinates: 57°17'54.0"N 7°11'35.0"W

Opened: 1857

Automated: 1970

Deactivated: Active

Height: 12 meters, 39 feet

Focal Height: 54 meters, 177 feet

Signal: White/red flash every 20 seconds

Foghorn signal: N/A

Visitor Access: Closed

Weavers Point Lighthouse, Outer Hebrides

There is limited information for this site. It was opened in 1980 as an automated light and is still active.

Description: White hut

Location: North Uist

Directions: Accessible by boat

Coordinates: 57°36'30.0"N 7°06'00.0"W

Opened: 1980

Automated: 1980

Deactivated: Active

Height: 7 meters, 23 feet

Focal Height: 21 meters, 70 feet

Signal: White flash every 3 seconds

Foghorn signal: N/A

Visitor Access: Closed

St. Abbs Lighthouse, Scottish Borders

After the sinking of the Martello on Carr Rock in 1857, the Northern Lighthouse Board recommended the building of a lighthouse at St Abb's Head. The lighthouse was built by Engineers David and Thomas Stevenson and the station opened in The lighthouse was built by Engineers David and Thomas Stevenson and the St Abb's Head Lighthouse was first lit in 1862. In 1876 a foghorn was added, the first for a Scottish lighthouse. The station was automated in 1993 and is still active.

Description: White tower and building

Location: St. Abb's Head

Directions: From Eyemouth, head northwest on an unnamed road for 1.5 miles and the site

Coordinates: 55°54'58.0"N 2°08'19.0"W

Opened: 1862

Automated: 1993

Deactivated: Active

Height: 9 meters, 30 feet

Focal Height: 68 meters, 223 feet

Signal: White flash every 10 seconds

Foghorn signal: Discontinued 1987 (Was 1 blast every 45 seconds)

Visitor Access: Closed

Firths Voe Lighthouse, Shetland

Firths Voe lighthouse was built to aid vessels through the narrow approach channel to Sullom Voe via the south east entrance into Yell Sound. The light was completed in 1909 by David and Charles Stevenson. The light is a small 8 metre high cast iron structure.

Description: White cylindrical tower

Location: Mainland

Directions: From the village of Mossbank, head south toward Maidenfield for 0.2 mi and turn left on unnamed road Drive 0.1 miles to the end of the road. The light is a short walk east near the coast.

Coordinates: 60°27'13.0"N 1°10'37.0"W

Opened: 1909

Automated: 1909

Deactivated: Active

Height: 8 meters, 26 feet

Focal Height: 9 meters, 29 feet

Signal: Occulting White/Red/Green every 8 sec

Foghorn signal: N/A

Visitor Access: Grounds open, tower closed

Bressay Lighthouse, Shetland

Bressay Lighthouse was built in Shetland in 1858 by brothers David Stevenson and Thomas Stevenson. It was lit by a paraffin vapour burner with a revolving optic powered by a falling weight. The area has still seen a number of shipping mishaps. In 1993 an oil tanker grounded nearby which had devastating effects on marine life. The same year saw a factory ship ground near the station.

Description: White cylindrical tower

Location: Bressay Island

Directions: Bressay is a 5 minute ferry ride from the Northlink ferry terminal on Mainland Shetland

Coordinates: 60°07'12.0"N 1°07'17.0"W

Opened: 1858

Automated: 1998

Deactivated: 2012

Height: 16 meters, 52 feet

Focal Height: 32 meters, 105 feet

Signal: 2 white flashes every 20 seconds

Foghorn signal: 2 blasts every 90 seconds, Discontinued 1987

Visitor Access: Tower closed, keepers dwellings can be rented

Esha Ness Lighthouse, Shetland

This was the last Northern Lighthouse Board lighthouse built by a member of the Stevenson family. It was built in 1929 by David Stevenson and was needed to warn ships of the Ve Skerries nearby. The lighthouse could not save the trawler Ben Doran which wrecked with all seamen lost shortly after the station opened.

Description: White square tower

Location: Mainland

Directions: From Stennis, head northeast on B9078 for 0.5 mi and turn left on an unnamed road and the site is 0.8 mi

Coordinates: 60°29'21.0"N 1°37'38.0"W

Opened: 1925

Automated: 1974

Deactivated: Active

Height: 12 meters, 39 feet

Focal Height: 61 meters, 200 feet

Signal: White flash every 12 seconds

Foghorn signal: N/A

Visitor Access: Closed

Fair Isle North Lighthouse, Shetland

Fair Isle North is one of two lighthouses built on Fair Isle By David and Charles Stevenson in 1892. At 14 meters, the North Lighthouse is much smaller as it sits on a 65 meter cliff. The station was attacked twice in 1942 with machine guns and bombs resulting in the destruction of outbuildings. The site was automated in 1983.

Description: White tower

Location: Fair Isle

Directions: From the ferry dock, head south on Fair Isle - Sumburgh Airport for 0.2 mi and turn right to stay on Fair Isle - Sumburgh Airport and reach the site in 1.6 miles

Coordinates: 59°33'08.0"N 1°36'35.0"W

Opened: 1892

Automated: 1983

Deactivated: Active

Height: 14 meters, 46 feet

Focal Height: 80 meters, 262 feet

Signal: 2 white flashes every 30 seconds

Foghorn signal: 3 blasts every 45 seconds

Visitor Access: Grounds open, tower closed

Fair Isle South Lighthouse, Shetland

Fair Isle South is one of two lighthouses built on Fair Isle By David and Charles Stevenson in 1892. At 26 meters, the South Lighthouse is much higher as it sits at a lower level. In 1941 the wife of the Assistant Lightkeeper was killed in an air attack and in 1942 the wife and daughter of the Principle Keeper were killed by bombs. The light was automated in 1998.

Description: White tower

Location: Fair Isle

Directions: From Stonybreck, head SW on Fair Isle - Sumburgh Airport for 1.0 miles and find the lighthouse

Coordinates: 59°30'50.0"N 1°39'10.0"W

Opened: 1892

Automated: 1998

Deactivated: Active

Height: 26 meters, 85 feet

Focal Height: 32 meters, 105 feet

Signal: 4 white flashes every 30 seconds

Foghorn signal: 2 blasts every 60 seconds

Visitor Access: Grounds open, tower closed

Foula Lighthouse, Shetland

The light on Foula Island was established due to an increase in oil tanker traffic using the west coast route. The light lens is a Fourth order Fresnel which was modified to metal halide lamps. The light was modified to run on solar power in 2000.

Description: White tower

Location: Foula Island

Directions: Accessible by boat

Coordinates: 60°06'45.0"N 2°03'50.0"W

Opened: 1986

Automated: 1986

Deactivated: Active

Height: 8 meters, 26 feet

Focal Height: 36 meters, 118 feet

Signal: 3 white flashes every 16 seconds

Foghorn signal: N/A

Visitor Access: Grounds open, tower closed

Muckle Flugga Lighthouse, Shetland

Mugga Flugga Lighthouse built by Thomas and David Stevenson and it is the most northerly light in the British Isles. A temporary light was established in 1854 but it was soon seen to be inadequate. The current lighthouse was opened in 1858 and was built to a high standard. This included sinking the foundation ten feet into the bedrock. In 1928 the lighting was changed from a fixed light to flashing. Muckle Flugga Lighthouse was automated in March 1995.

Description: White tower

Location: Muckle Flugga Island

Directions: Accessible by boat

Coordinates: 60°51'19.0"N 0°53'07.0"W

Opened: 1858

Automated: 1995

Deactivated: Active

Height: 20 meters, 66 feet

Focal Height: 66 meters, 217 feet

Signal: White flash every 20 seconds

Foghorn signal: N/A

Visitor Access: Closed

Bound Skerry Lighthouse, Shetland

David and Thomas Stevenson built the Bound Skerry Lighthouse in 1854 at the eastern port of Scotland. Like other Shetland lighthouses, it was attacked in WW2. In 1941 the station was machine gunned with little damage. However in 1942 it was bombed and the boatman's mother suffered fatal injuries. The station was automated in 1972.

Description: White cylindrical tower

Location: Bound Skerry

Directions: Accessible by boat

Coordinates: 60°25'28.0"N 0°43'41.0"W

Opened: 1854

Automated: 1972

Deactivated: Active

Height: 33 meters, 108 feet

Focal Height: 44 meters, 144 feet

Signal: Flashing white every 20 seconds

Foghorn signal: N/A

Visitor Access: Closed

Point of Fethaland Lighthouse, Shetland

This light was built to guide tankers to the oil terminal at Sullom Voe near Firths Voe. It is located on Fethaland, a narrow peninsula at the north of the mainland. To reach the site, drive till road end and take either the coastal path or a farm track.

Description: White tower

Location: Mainland

Directions: From Isbister on the Mainland, head north on an unnamed road for 1.6 miles. Park and walk north for 150 feet to find the light.

Coordinates: 60°38'03.0"N 1°18'41.0"W

Opened: 1977

Automated: 1977

Deactivated: Active

Height: 7 meters, 23 feet

Focal Height: 65 meters, 213 feet

Signal: 3 flashes every 15 seconds, white or red depending on direction

Foghorn signal: N/A

Visitor Access: Grounds only

Sumburgh Head Lighthouse, Shetland

The Sumburgh Head Light was built by Robert Stevenson in 1821 and it is the oldest lighthouse in Shetland. Sumburgh Head is an important nesting site for seabirds and the station is headquarters for the Sumburgh Head Nature Reserve. Overnight accommodations are available. In 1820, as the station was being built, the ship Freemason was carrying in materials. It wrecked nearby and only one seaman was saved. There is an excellent visitor centre at the site.

Description: White cylindrical tower

Location: Mainland

Directions: From Grutness at the southern tip of the Mainland, walk south along Sumburgh Head Lane for 1.5 miles and see the site

Coordinates: 59°51'14.0"N 1°16'29.0"W

Opened: 1821

Automated: 1991

Deactivated: Active

Height: 17 meters, 56 feet

Focal Height: 91 meters, 299 feet

Signal: 3 white flashes every 20 seconds

Foghorn signal: 1 blast every 90 seconds

Visitor Access: The keeper's dwelling is available to rent

Ailsa Craig Lighthouse, South Ayrshire

Ailsa Craig Lighthouse is located on Ailsa Craig, an island in the Firth of Clyde, just offshore from Girvan, South Ayrshire, Scotland. The lighthouse was established in 1886 by Thomas and David A Stevenson. Two substantial foghorns with concrete housings were built at the same time. The lighthouse was automated in 1990 and converted to solar power in 2001. The island is a bird sanctuary featuring kittiwakes, gannets and puffins.

Description: White tower

Location: Ailsa Craig

Directions: Accessible by boat

Coordinates: 55°15'06.0"N 5°06'24.0"W

Opened: 1886

Automated: 1990

Deactivated: Active

Height: 11 meters, 36 feet

Focal Height: 18 meters, 59 feet

Signal: White flash every 4 seconds

Foghorn signal: Discontinued 1987 (Was 3 blasts of 3 seconds, every 45 seconds)

Visitor Access: Closed

Lady Isle Lighthouse, South Ayrshire

Lady Isle is a small, uninhabited island, in the Firth of Clyde. Lady Isle Lighthouse. Lady Isle Lighthouse was designed by David Alan Stevenson and Charles Stevenson and opened in 1903. It was built to warn ships of the island itself as well as Half Tide Rock and Scart Rock to the northeast. It is unique in having a spiral staircase which is open on the side of the tower. The light was automated in 2004 and is still active.

Description: White tower

Location: Lady Isle

Directions: Accessible by boat

Coordinates: 55°31'38.0"N 4°44'02.0"W

Opened: 1903

Automated: 2004

Deactivated: Active

Height: 15 meters, 49 feet

Focal Height: 19 meters, 62 feet

Signal: White flash every 2 seconds

Foghorn signal: Deactivated

Visitor Access: Closed

Turnberry Lighthouse, South Ayrshire and Kirkoswald

Bristo Rock, near Turnberry Point, had been the cause of so many shipwrecks that in 1869 it was proposed that a lighthouse be built. The Turnberry Lighthouse was designed by engineers David and Thomas Stevenson with John Barr as the contractor. The station opened in 1873. The lighthouse was automated in 1986 and converted to solar power in 2013. It continues to be active.

Description: White tower

Location: Turnberry Point

Directions: From Turnberry, head north on Maidens Rd/A719 and continue to follow A719. After 0.7 mi turn left on unnamed road and the site is 0.7 miles

Coordinates: 55°19'33.0"N 4°50'41.0"W

Opened: 1873

Automated: 1986

Deactivated: Active

Height: 24 meters, 79 feet

Focal Height: 29 meters, 95 feet

Signal: White flash every 15 seconds

Foghorn signal: N/A

Visitor Access: Closed

Holborn Head Lighthouse, Thurso

The Board of Trade granted permission for a lighthouse to be built at Holborn Head but due to budget squabbles, it was not completed until 1862. It was designed and built by David and Thomas Stevenson with the contractor being Mr Stewart from Peterhead. The light was automated in 1988 and deactivated in 2003.

Description: White tower joined to building

Location: Holburn Head

Directions: From Scrabster, head northeast on an unnamed road for 0.2 miles and find the site

Coordinates: 58°36'53.0"N 3°32'22.0"W

Opened: 1862

Automated: 1988

Deactivated: 2003

Height: 17 meters, 56 feet

Focal Height: 23 meters, 75 feet

Signal: Flashing White/Red every 10 Seconds

Foghorn signal: Discontinued 1987 (Was 1 blast every 20 seconds)

Visitor Access: Grounds open, tower closed

Aberdeenshire Tour

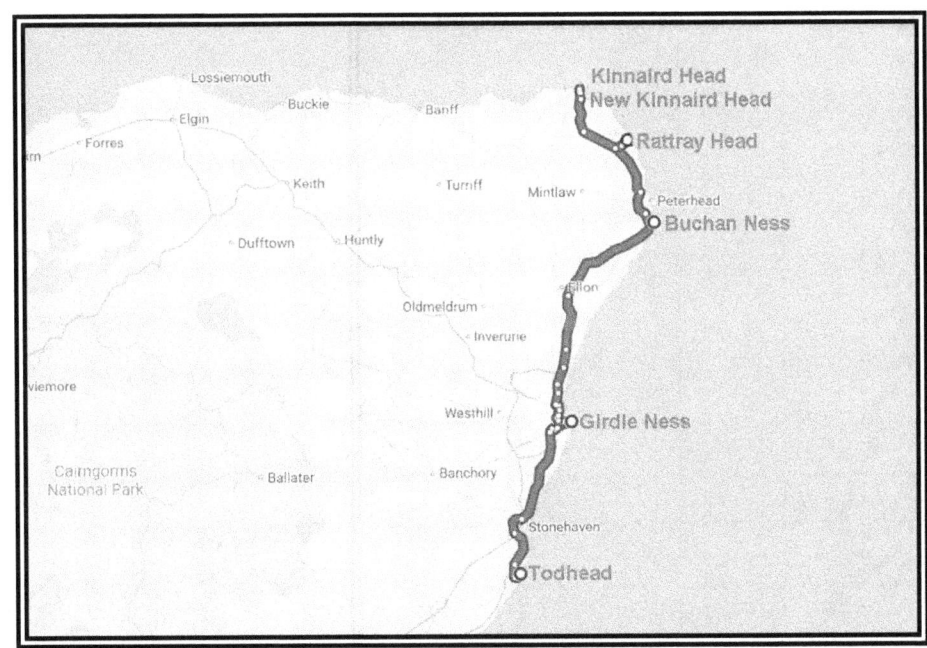

6 lighthouses, 2.5 hours driving

Todhead Lighthouse	56°53'02.0"N 2°12'55.0"W
Girdle Ness Lighthouse	57°08'20.0"N 2°02'55.0"W
Buchan Ness Lighthouse	57°28'13.0"N 1°46'28.0"W
Rattray Head lighthouse	57°36'36.0"N 1°48'59.0"W
New Kinnaird Head Lighthouse	57°41'53.0"N 2°00'15.0"W
Kinnaird Head Lighthouse	57°41'53.0"N 2°00'15.0"W

Dumfries and Galloway Tour

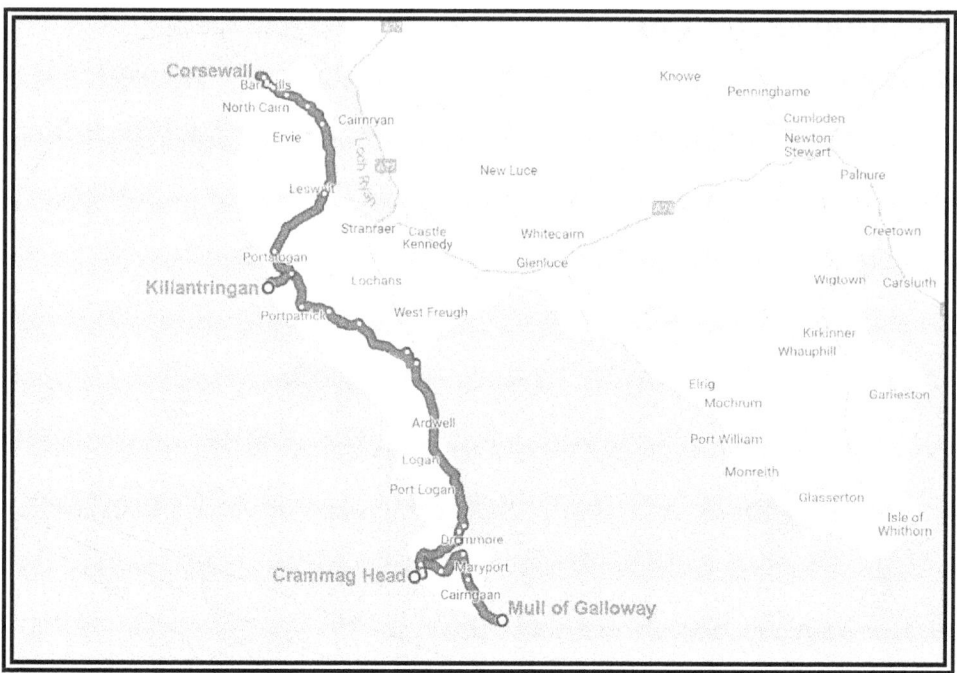

4 Lighthouses, 1 hour 45 minutes driving

Mull of Galloway Lighthouse	54°38'06.0"N 4°51'26.0"W
Crammag Head Lighthouse	54°39'53.0"N 4°57'54.0"W
Killantringan Lighthouse	54°51'42.0"N 5°08'49.0"W
Corsewall Lighthouse	55°00'25.0"N 5°09'33.0"W

East Coast Tour

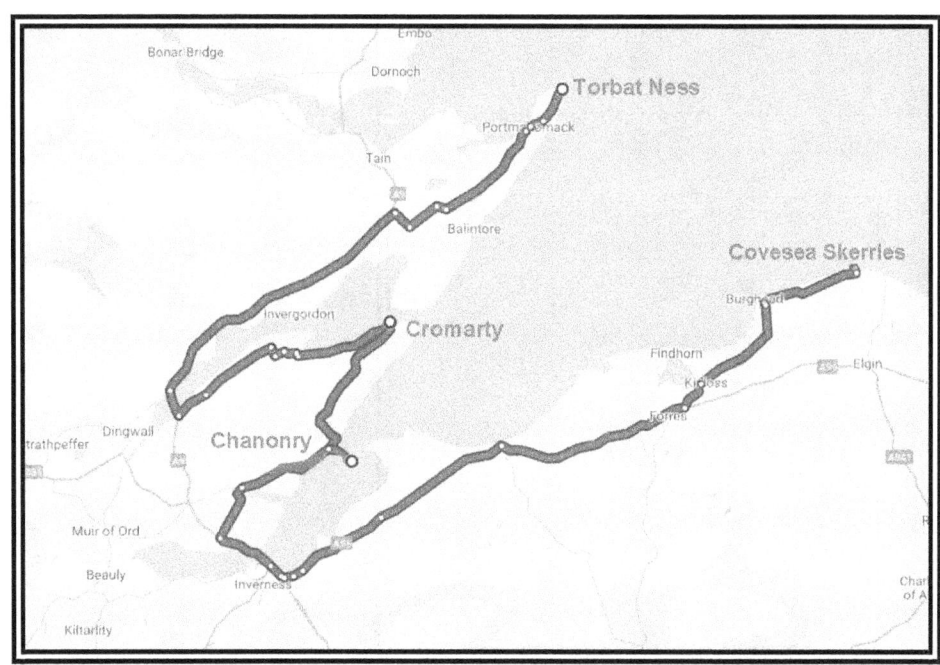

4 Lighthouses, 3 hours driving

Torbat Ness Lighthouse	57°51'54.0"N 3°46'36.0"W
Cromarty Lighthouse	57°40'59.0"N 4°02'11.0"W
Chanonry Lighthouse	57°34'26.0"N 4°05'34.0"W
Covesea Skerries Lighthouse	57°43'27.0"N 3°20'19.0"W

Isle of May Tour

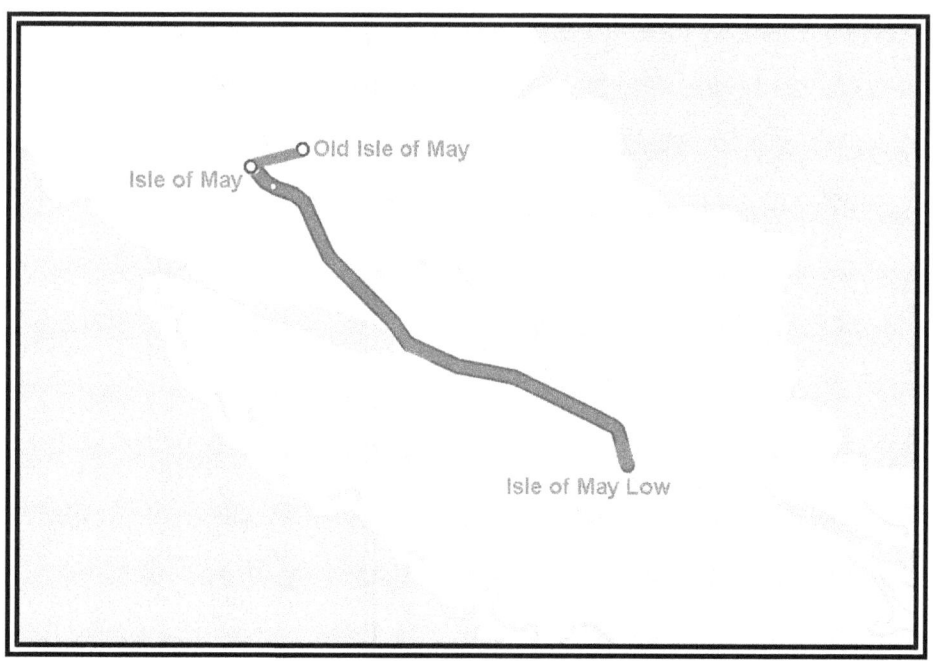

3 lighthouse, 15 minutes walking

Old Isle of May Lighthouse   56°11'09.0"N 2°33'24.0"W
Isle of May Lighthouse   56°11'08.0"N 2°33'27.0"W
Isle of May Low Light   56°10'59.0"N 2°33'07.0"W

The Isle of May is accessible by ferry from Anstruther, Crail, or North Berwick

North Coast Tour

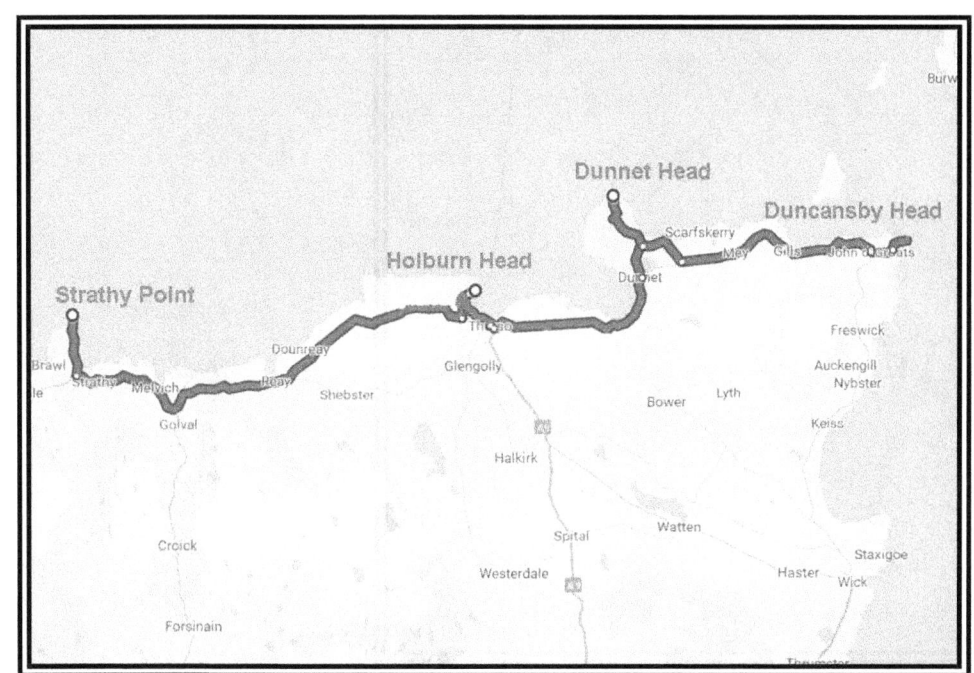

4 Lighthouses, 2 hours driving

Strathy Point Lighthouse	58°35'55.0"N 4°01'07.0"W
Holburn Head Lighthouse	58°36'52.1"N 3°32'22.1"W
Dunnet Head Lighthouse	58°40'17.0"N 3°22'35.0"W
Duncansby Head Lighthouse	58°38'38.0"N 3°01'31.0"W

Southwest Coast Tour

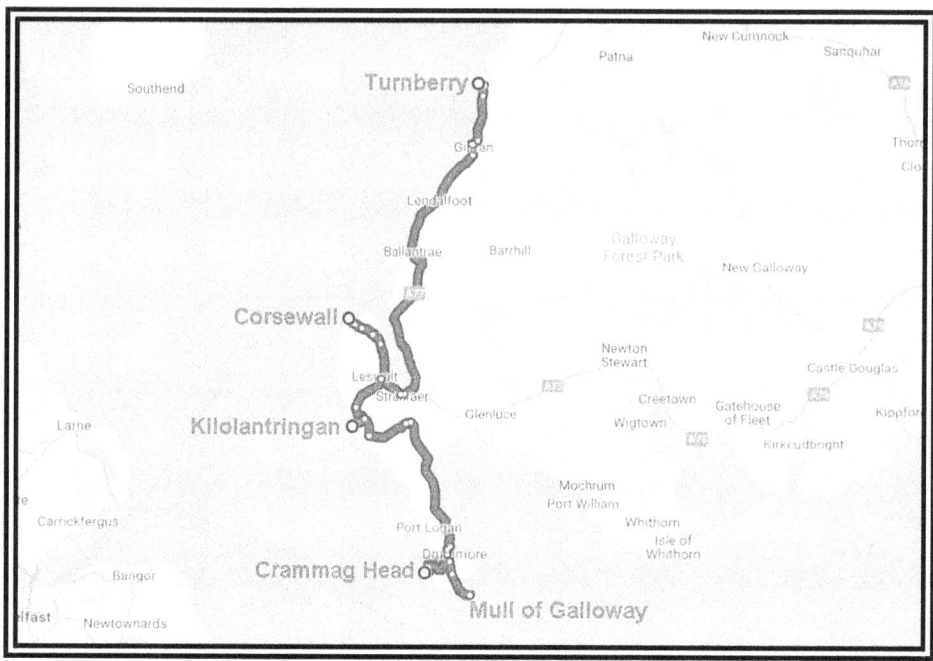

5 Lighthouses, 3 hours driving

Turnberry Lighthouse   55°19'33.0"N 4°50'41.0"W
Corsewall Lighthouse   55°00'25.0"N 5°09'33.0"W
Killantringan Lighthouse   54°51'42.0"N 5°08'49.0"W
Crammag Head Lighthouse   54°39'53.0"N 4°57'54.0"W
Mull of Galloway Lighthouse   54°38'06.0"N 4°51'26.0"W

Glossary of Lighthouse Terms

Aerobeacon: A lighting system which creates a signal over long distances. It consists of a strong light source with a focusing mechanism which is rotated on a vertical axis. It has been used at airports as well as lighthouses.

Acetylene: After 1910, acetylene began to be used to power the lighthouse light source. It has the advantage that it could be stored on site with a sun valve turning it on at dusk and off at daybreak.

Alternating Light: A light source which changes colours in a regular pattern.

Arc of Visibility: The range of the horizon from which the lighthouse is visible from the sea.

Automated: A lighthouse that operates without a keeper. The light functions are controlled by timers, and light and fog detectors.

Beacon: A fixed aid to navigation.

Bell: A sound signal produced by fixed aids and by sea movement on buoys.

Breakwater: A structure that protects a shore area or harbour by blocking waves.

Bull's-eye Lens: A convex lens used to refract light.

Catwalk: An elevated walkway which allows the keeper to move in the lantern room in towers built in the sea.

Characteristic: The distinct pattern of the flashing light or foghorn blast which allows seamen to distinguish which light station it is coming from.

Chariot: A wheeled assembly at the bottom of a Fresnel lens which is rotated around a circular track.

Clockwork Mechanism: Early lighthouses had a series of gears, pulleys and weights, which had to be wound on a recurring basis by the keepers.

Cottage Style Lighthouse: A lighthouse made up of a keeper's residence with a light on top.

Crib: A base structure filled with stone which acted as the foundation for the structure built on top.

Daymark: A unique colour pattern that identifies a specific lighthouse during the day.

Decommissioned: A lighthouse that has discontinued operating as a aid to navigation.

Diaphone: A sound signal produced by a slotted piston moved by compressed air.

Directional Light: A light which marks the direction to be followed.

Eclipse: The interval between light flashed or foghorn blasts.

Fixed Light: A light shining continuously without periods of eclipse or darkness.

Flashing Light: Alight pattern distinguished by periods of eclipse or darkness.

Focal Plane: The path of a beam of light emitted from a lighthouse. The height from the center of the beam to the sea is known as the height of the focal plane.

Fog Detector: A device used to automatically determine conditions which may reduce visibility and the need to start a sound signal.

Fog Signal: An audible device such as a bell or horn that warns seamen during period of fog when the light would be ineffective.

Fresnel Lens: An optic system composed of a convex lens and prisms which concentrate the light beam through a series of prisms. The design was produced by Augustin Fresnel in the 1800s.

Geographic Range: The longest distance the curvature of the earth allows an object of a certain height to be seen.

Isophase Light: A light in which the duration of light and darkness are equal.

Keeper: The person responsible for the maintenance and operation of the lighthouse.

Lamp and Reflector: A lamp and polished mirror used before the invention of more effective optic systems such as the Fresnel lens.

Lantern: A glass covered space at the top of the lighthouse tower, which housed the lighting equipment.

Lens: The glass optical system used to concentrate and direct the light.

Light Sector: The arc over which a light can be seen from the sea.

Lightship: A ship that served as a lighthouse.

Light Station: The lighthouse tower as well as any outbuildings such as the keeper's quarters, fog-signal building, fuel storage building and boathouse.

Nautical Mile: A unit of distance which is the average distance on the Earth's surface represented by one minute of latitude. It is equal to 1.1508 statute miles and mainly used at sea.

Nominal Range: The distance a light can be seen in good weather.

Occulting Light: A light in which the period of light is longer than the period of darkness and in which the intervals of darkness are all equal. Also known as an eclipsing light.

Order: A description of the power of the Fresnel lens ranging from one to seven from stronger to weaker.

Parabolic Reflector: A metal bowl shaped to a parabolic curve which reflects a lamp's light from it's center.

Parapet: A railed walkway which surrounds the lamp room.

Period: The total time for one cycle of the pattern of the light or sound signal.

Pharologist: A person with an interest in lighthouses.

Range Lights: Two lights which form a range provide direction to mariners for safe passage. They are described as the Front and Rear Lighthouses or the Inner and Outer. The front range light is lower than the rear, and when they align, the ship is in the proper position.

Revetment: A bank of stone laid to protect a structure against erosion from waves.

Revolving Light: A flash produced by the rotation of a Fresnel lens.

Riprap: Broken rocks or stone placed to help prevent erosion.

Sector: The portion of the sea lit by a sector light.

Skeleton Tower: Towers consisting of four or more braced feet with a beacon on top. They have little resistance to the wind and waves, and bear up well in a storm.

Solar-powered Optic: Many automated lights are run on solar powered batteries.

Spider Lamp: A brass container holding oil and solid wicks.

Tender: A ship which services lighthouses.

Ventilator: Opening' at the top of a lighthouse tower to provide heat exhaust and air flow within the tower.

Wick Solid: A solid cord which draws fuel to the flame in spider lamps.

Photo Credits

Alessio Damato, Tower of Hercules; **Alan Jamieson**, Buchan Ness; **Andy Stephonson**, Calf of Man Lower, **August Schwerdfeger**, Lismore, **Barry Boxer,** Crammag Head; **Becky Williamson**, Ruvaal; **Beth Loft**, Start Point; **Bill Boaden**, Hoxa Head; **Bill Harrison**, Kinnaird Old, Kinnaird New, **Boakesey**, Calf of Man Outer, Calf of Man New; **Bob Jones**, Barra Head, Monarch Isles Old, Monarch Isles New; **Calum McRoberts**, Tor Ness, Rona; **Chris Downer**, Bound Skerry, Scarinish, Tiumpian; **Colin**, Rubha nan Gall, **Dave Conner**, Chanonry; **Dave Simpson**, Copinsay; **Alessio Damato**, Tower of Hercules; **Alan Jamieson**, Buchan Ness; **Andy Stephonson**, Calf of Man Lower; **August Schwerdfeger**, Lismore; **Barry Boxer**, Crammag Head; **Becky Williamson**, Ruvaalp; **Beth Loft**, Start Point; **Bill Boaden**, Hoxa Head; **Bill Harrison**, Kinnaird Old, Kinnaird New; **Boakesey**, Calf of Man Outer, Calf of Man New; **Bob Jones**, Barra Head, Monarch Isles Old, Monarch Isles New; **Calum McRoberts**, Tor Ness, Rona; **Chris Downer**, Bound Skerry, Scarinish, Tiumpian; **Colin**, Rubha nan Gallp; **Dave Conner**, Chanonry; **Dave Simpson**, Copinsay; **David Dixon**, Killantringan, Point of Ayre Lights; **David Stanley**, Isle May Low; **Donald MacDonald**, DubhArtach; **Doug Lee**, Cumbrae; **Fabio Sassi**, Hoy High, Hoy Low; **Gestumblindl**, Holburn Head; **Ian Balcombe**, Auskerry; **James Allan**, Weavers Point; **JBellis**, Noup Head; **Jim Bain**, Elie Ness; **JJM**, Flannan Isles; **John Tustin**, Dennis Head, North Ronaldsay; **Julian Paren**, Foula; **L J Cunningham**, Holy Island Inner; **Marinas**, McArthurs Head; **Mary and Angus Hogg**, Corsewell; **Michael Earnshaw**, Sule Skerry; **Mike Pennington**, Firths Voe, **Odd Wellies**, Hyskeir; **Raibeart MacAoidh**, Cumbrae Little; **Reading Tom**, Carraig Fhadap; **Richard Allan**, Waterness; **Richard Webb**, Little Cumbrae New. **Roddy MacDonald**, North Rona; **Ron Ireland**, Fair Isle South; **Rosser1954**, Lady Isle; **Rude Health**, Ailsa Craig; **S McKechnie**, Turnberry; **ScottishAttractions**, Fidra; **secretlondon123**, Holy Isle Outer; **Thiersch,** Pharos **Thomas Keetley**, Rinns of Islay; **Unukorno**, Esha Ness; **Verisimilus**, Muckle Fulga

All Other Images by the author

The Photographer's and Explorer's Series

Unless noted, there are Print and eBook editions available for the following.

Birding Guide to Orkney
Guide to Photographing Birds

Maine Lighthouses
Ontario Lighthouses
Orkney and Shetland Lighthouses
Lighthouses of Scotland

Ontario's Old Mills
Ontario Waterfalls

Alabama Covered Bridges (eBook)
Covered bridges of Canada
California Covered Bridges (eBook)
Connecticut Covered Bridges (eBook)
Georgia Covered Bridges (eBook)
Illinois Covered Bridges (eBook)
Indiana Covered Bridges
Iowa Covered Bridges (eBook)
Maine Covered Bridges (eBook)
Massachusetts Covered Bridges (eBook)
Michigan Covered Bridges (eBook)
New Brunswick Covered Bridges
New England Covered Bridges
Covered Bridges of the Mid-Atlantic
Covered Bridges of the South
New Hampshire Covered Bridges
New York Covered Bridges
Ohio's Covered Bridges
Oregon Covered Bridges
Quebec Covered bridges
The Covered Bridges of Kentucky (eBook)
The Covered Bridges of Kentucky and Tennessee
The Covered Bridges of Tennessee (eBook)
Vermont's Covered Bridges
The Covered Bridges of Virginia (eBook)
The Covered Bridges of Virginia and West Virginia
The Covered Bridges of West Virginia (eBook)
Washington Covered Bridges (eBook)
Wisconsin Covered Bridges (eBook)

Index

Ailsa Craig Lighthouse	113
Ardnamurchan Lighthouse	56
Auskerry Lighthouse	83
Barns Ness Lighthouse	41
Barra Head Lighthouse	96
Bass Rock Lighthouse	42
Bell Rock Lighthouse	19
Bound Skerry Lighthouse	110
Bressay Lighthouse	104
Brough of Birsay Lighthouse	84
Buchan Ness Lighthouse	15
Butt of Lewis Lighthouse	97
Cantick Head Lighthouse	85
Cape Wrath Lighthouse	57
Carraig Fhada Lighthouse	23
Chanonry Lighthouse	69
Cloch Lighthouse	70
Copinsay Lighthouse	86
Corran Point Lighthouse	51
Corsewall Lighthouse	36
Covesea Skerries Lighthouse	71
Crammag Head Lighthouse	37
Cromarty Lighthouse	58
Cumbrae Lighthouse	73
Davaar Lighthouse	24
Dennis Head Old Beacon	81
Dubh Artach Lighthouse	25
Duncansby Head Lighthouse	59
Dunnet Head Lighthouse	52
Eilean Glas Lighthouse	98
Elie Ness Lighthouse	44
Esha Ness Lighthouse	105
Fair Isle North Lighthouse	106
Fair Isle South Lighthouse	107
Fethaland Lighthouse	111
Fidra Lighthouse	43
Fife Ness Lighthouse	47
Firths Voe Lighthouse	103
Flannan Isles Lighthouse	93
Foula Lighthouse	108

Girdle Ness Lighthouse	14
Girdleness Lighthouse	14
Holborn Head Lighthouse	116
Holy Isle Inner Lighthouse	75
Holy Isle Outer Lighthouse	76
Hoxa Head Lighthouse	87
Hoy Sound High Light	78
Hoy Sound Low Light	79
Hyskeir Lighthouse	60
Inchkeith Lighthouse	48
Isle of May Lighthouse	49
Isle of May Low Light	50
Killantringan Lighthouse	38
Kinnaird Head Lighthouse	16
Lady Isle Lighthouse	114
Lismore Lighthouse	26
Little Cumbrae New Lighthouse	74
Little Cumbrae Old Lighthouse	72
Little Ross lighthouse	39
Loch Indaal Lighthouse	27
Lother Rock Light	88
McArthur's Head Lighthouse	28
Muckle Flugga Lighthouse	109
Mull of Galloway Lighthouse	35
Mull of Kintyre Lighthouse	29
Neist Point Lighthouse	61
New Kinnaird Head Lighthouse	16
New Monach Light	99
North Rona Lighthouse	94
North Ronaldsay Lighthouse	80
Noss Head Lighthouse	62
Noup Head Lighthouse	89
Old Isle of May Lighthouse	45
Old Monach Lighthouse	99
Ornsay Lighthouse	63
Oxcars Lighthouse	46
Pentland Skerries High Light	90
Pladda Lighthouse	77
Point of Sleat Lighthouse	64
Rattray Head lighthouse	17
Rinns of Islay Lighthouse	30
Rona Lighthouse	65
Rua Reidh Lighthouse	66

Rubha nan Gall Lighthouse	21
Ruvaal Lighthouse	34
Sanda Island Lighthouse	31
Scarinish Lighthouse	32
Scurdie Ness Lighthouse	20
Skerryvore Lighthouse	33
Southerness Lighthouse	40
St. Abbs Lighthouse	102
Start Point Lighthouse	82
Stoer Head Lighthouse	67
Strathy Point Lighthouse	68
Stroma Lighthouse	53
Sule Skerry Lighthouse	91
Sumburgh Head Lighthouse	112
Tarbat Ness Lighthouse	54
Tiumpan Head Lighthouse	95
Todhead Lighthouse	18
Tor Ness Lighthouse	92
Toward Point Lighthouse	22
Turnberry Lighthouse	115
Ushenish Lighthouse	100
Vaternish Lighthouse	55
Weavers Point Lighthouse	101

www.ingramcontent.com/pod-product-compliance
Lightning Source LLC
Chambersburg PA
CBHW080557090426
42735CB00016B/3270